Meta-Verse!*

it's going to be interesting to see how yesterday goes

a coloring, pick-your-own poem, space-time romp
exploring pandemic, parenting, politics, personal, past

Joann Renee Boswell

illustrations by Jay Williams & Joey Hartmann-Dow

*no relation to the recently renamed social media giant

Fernwood
PRESS

Meta-Verse!

it's going to be interesting to see how yesterday goes

Fernwood Press
Newberg, Oregon
www.fernwoodpress.com

Printed in the United States of America

Cover and page design: Mareesa Fawver Moss
Cover photo: NASA via Unsplash
Author photo: Mark Pratt-Russum

ISBN 978-1-59498-105-0

Reader, the book you're holding is unlike any poetry collection you've ever met before. This is a guidebook for living fully in the most turbulent moments of our lifetime. This is a coloring book because you too are the artist, and every day is another chance to create beauty. This is a mirror, because while each piece is deeply personal for the author, you'll see yourself in these poems as you choose your path through the wonder and anxiety of living in a universe where "each step / uncertain and tender" is still yours to make. Most importantly, this collection is a reminder that, in whatever universe you find yourself, you are the chooser. Boswell challenges you to choose the path toward peace, awe, and love. Take her up on this journey and be transformed.

Armin Tolentino
Clark County Poet Laureate (2021–2023),
author of *We Meant to Bring It Home Alive*

In her latest collection, Joann Renee Boswell invites us to leap with her into the "multidimensional wormhole" of the metaverse, a choose-your-own-adventure coloring book version of this life in which "we are / magnificent. / complex." A fearless, capable guide, Boswell believes in our ability to stay with her as she careens from parenting to self-love to quantum physics, from the injustices of racism, sexism, fascism, and religious hypocrisy to the liberatory mysticism of art and magic. We are even encouraged to draw on the pages without illustrations, for "there's always space for more creative chaos." Prepare yourself for a fun, engaging, and transformative dive into this poet's multitudinous and ever-expanding consciousness. You'll be glad you played along.

Christopher Luna
Clark County Poet Laureate (2013–2017),
author of *Voracity*

Meta-Verse! is more than a book of poems, it's an adventure. Jo is creative, witty, and charming as she uses her poetry to guide us on a journey in, around, and through an expansive understanding of the world around us. The myriad ways to approach this work, especially with the bonus coloring content, allow readers to have a new experience every time we engage. You don't want to miss this unique insight into family, love, relationships, pandemic life, and so much more.

Meghan Crozier
author of *The Pursuing Life*
and co-host of Thereafter Podcast

Joann Boswell's *Meta-Verse!* is whimsical reading that packs a punch, including poems both unflinching and warmly invitational. As a poet, Boswell is equally adept at exploring realities that disappoint and overwhelm (like parenting, politics, racism, restrictive religion, and lack of affordable housing) and finding—or manifesting—magic, especially magic in the self. For instance, she delights with an ode to her own legs (naming them her "Summer Crush") and a vivid, liberatory recounting of the first time wearing a crop top, which celebrates a stomach's "dimply radiance." Through *Meta-Verse!*, let Boswell introduce you to the "Goddess" who is "swallowing each ultimatum we waltz in," to the woman who is thankful "for not forgetting me," and to an existence of "chronic delight / paired with decay." By book's end, you might find yourself better primed to look for that "grasp of Glitter / always available" in each one of us and to name some uncomfortable truths!

Megan McDermott
author of *Jesus Merch: A Catalog in Poems*

for the scientists
the teachers
the artists
the medical professionals
you

timeline

introduction

I nearly named this book just straight up "Meta-Verse," but then my husband got a concussion, and during his recovery, while the kids were banging about the house after dinner, he said to me: "Well, it'll be interesting to see how yesterday goes." And I knew immediately that those words belonged with this manuscript.

I'd been working with the title "Meta-Verse" for six months, but I kept questioning it, pleading with it to tell me: Wasn't that title just a wee too meta? Too inaccessible? Too bizarre? But the manuscript never answered, so I kept cutting poems and revising lines and chopping up stanzas, waiting for the miracle of inspiration.

You see, back when the concept of the book was coming together, I was listening to the prologue for a *This American Life* podcast episode (number 691) on my morning walk downtown for coffee and steps on my fitbit. I like to reach five thousand steps by 9:30 a.m. (I'm no David Sedaris.) This particular episode began by talking about how the multiverse works. I'd synthesize it for you, but I wouldn't do it justice. Here, take a few minutes and go find it. The intro (which is all you need) is short and mind-melting. I'll wait.

Welcome back into whatever multiverse you are in where you are holding this book.

I had just reached the coffee shop to order my one-pump peppermint americano with cream when I finished that portion of the episode. The barista had clearly forgotten my name (that she'd just learned the previous week). I quickly forgave her, realizing that this was a trick of the multiverse, and somewhere out there was a barista who did remember my name. Probably in that other universe, I'd forgotten that her name is Bailey.

So, we find ourselves here, in this book where you can split the meta-verse as often as you'd like, jumping around the various poems that I wrote during the pandemic. These poems reflect what my life was during those first fifteen months: scattered, overwhelmed, whimsical, nostalgic, pissed, political, exhausted, diseased, smitten.

You may, of course, read straight through (if you dare), but if you do jump around, please go ahead and mark off your journey in the TIMELINE (table of contents). Yes, write in this book! Go ahead! In fact, this is a coloring book! Please add life to the brilliant illustrations that Joey Hartmann-Dow and Jay Williams created for this book. And the few poems that have no illustrations to accompany them, please draw your own! Crowd these pages. There's always space for more creative chaos.

To begin, please go to the next page to read the titular poem.

Ready, Set, Engage!

Meta-Verse

in this iteration of earth
barista Bailey calls me "Girl!"
three times in one minute
clearly can't recall my name
because split universe Bailey
took that memory with her

———

each decision is a mirror
whirling quantum mechanic
goddess governing the very small
every spark of light
subject still to math
this single photon takes multiple paths

but we find it only once here
the left or right of it illogically vanished
stolen into a new sacred other:
our world copied
with just this one difference
and then another, infinity duplicates

expanding with each choice
parallel dimensions winking
such flirtation with could-have
reflections, an echo of multiverse
we swoon, subjects of physics
our fates, just hide-and-seek children

———

and now I see you hover
wondering if you *can*—
spoiler: you didn't buy this book
in the split universe
where barista Bailey knows my name
so you have to now, in *this* one

Continue to the next page.

frantic octopus

Guests

—for Lorelei

we unfurl, a tornado
persuaded to dump
our belongings upon
your sofa, spilling
over each square inch
flooding the floor
family of five storm
your one bedroom
overlooking Deschutes
River. the liquor
stand potions glimmer
tiny glass cups enchant
kids expect playthings
we whisper, *"Not for you!"*

NOT
FOR
YOU

Succumb: An Underwater Confessional

—for all the bozzytots, but particularly Renee (6-1/2 years old)

spiral down
the great staircase
of cat toys, marbles
balled up dirty socks
only worn for seventeen
minutes before she roasts
kicks them off, twisting
to the bathroom, abandons
her hoodie, then decides she's cold—
and off to procure more
socks and hoodies pulled
clean from drawers now dripping
items that dared be on top
of more preferred clothing articles—
the pinks and purples across the house
the grays and browns puddled
around her bereft dresser
a churning maelstrom rising—
I sink to the bottom, frantic octopus
wishing water wasn't quite this wet
lob these great limbs
sweeping displaced art—
bellowing underwater
makes but a gurgle—
she giggles, popping
my rage bubbles—
I'd like to stop—spiral *up*
let the undertow be
float on a sea of debris
succumb to wild

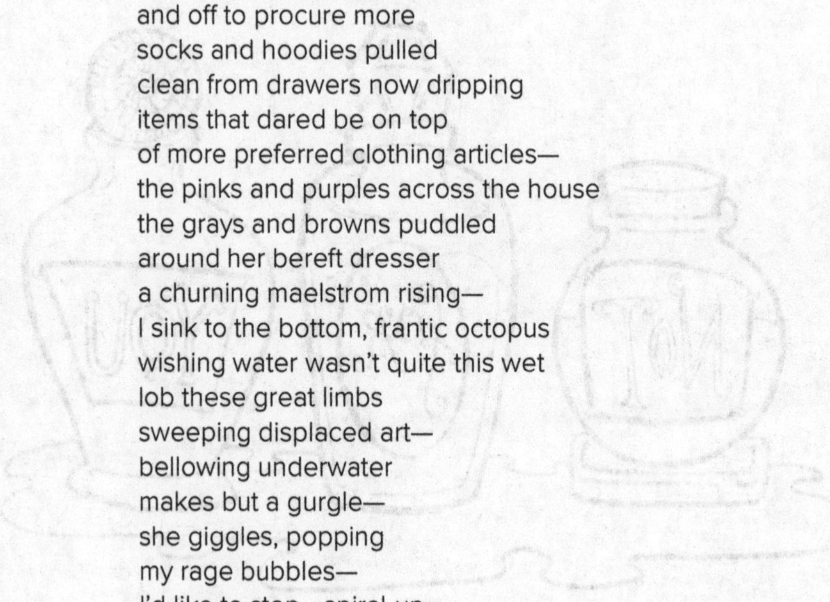

but I've yet to find the switch
to make my brain jelly-
fish, fluid and free
from the pain of coral Lego

        the flip that would render me relaxed
                in an open-floor plan with mermaid
        fin blankets taped to the cat tree
the desirable button that paints
my face with smiles so Cheshire
that even I believe myself blissful
or just slightly tolerant at sandy muffin
crumb surprises on the couch

                        so sorry, kid, pick up after yourself
                        or brace for twisted Calypso cries

!?!
I ♥ my mommy

Vertical-Lift Bridge

my atheist brother
and I began talking

our conservative
upbringing. silent

shared queries.
what connects

past to present
future predictions

we ask more now
than we did as kids

the bridge is up
traffic piles. water

flaunts freedom. we
submerge. talk for hours

what even *is* human?
this bridge spanning states—

how?!   we are
magnificent. complex

beyond comprehension. wonder
ruptures us silent. witness

miracle of innovation
like Saul on the road

to Damascus, we see
in a flash. our existence

astounds. are we *really*
here—the atheist and his big-skeptical

sister-mystic? and
what is God anyway?

my inability to cope
with chaos? the Universe?

that blade of grass
I just stepped on?

simply Love?

To swirl back through time and remember more familial relationships, go to page 47.
If the magnitude of the universe is making you feel so very tiny, go to page 77.
If the magnitude of the universe is making you feel warm and fuzzy and filled with mystical love, go to page 243.

bathed boreal,
I roar

Earthing

> *"'Dear old world,' she murmured, 'you are very lovely, and I am glad to be alive in you.'"*
> –L.M. Montgomery

> *"Walk as if you are kissing the Earth with your feet."*
> —Thich Nhat Hanh

> *"This a wonderful day. I've never seen this one before."*
> —Maya Angelou

Mama, I'm ashamed
these garments hinder
our embrace buried
with distrust and fear.
if I slip down nude
my body, pearls unstrung
careening slick, aware
magnetic—mammal waterfall—
can I feel   grass soft as skin?
those blades, milk between my toes
sweep up my spine, deep cleanse.
your greening answers homesick keening
the salmon beating ruby red raw—
damn obstacles dam-up return.
I let progress colonialize my ass
synthetic poly-fibers suffocate
peaches tumble overboard, shrink-wrapped
peel back this humidity
roll my humanity, all at sea
in fields bathed boreal, I roar
my weird—corporeal call quickens
natural verdure, earthen mermaid
my backbone is fern
bending with breeze
flexible jade release
with the light, curl
connected
kissed
home

Sexy Stranger

"If women farted as freely as men,
perhaps the appeal would wear off."
—me

every time you *ogle*
eye-snacking my ass
I let it rip

summon the beans
and greens of last night's bowl
cruciferous might

fill my body with sky
puffing my chest
like provocative clouds

posed perfection, one toe tipped
twist chin over shoulder
flash you

the flirtiest smile, an invitation
extended magnanimously
for you to linger

like the air at the top of the stairs
that clings desperately to the culmination
of kitchen and bathroom

once you're glued, I push
rank cloud through my breathable
yoga pants

write *broccoli* on my palm
and wave my perfume
to your gaping mouth

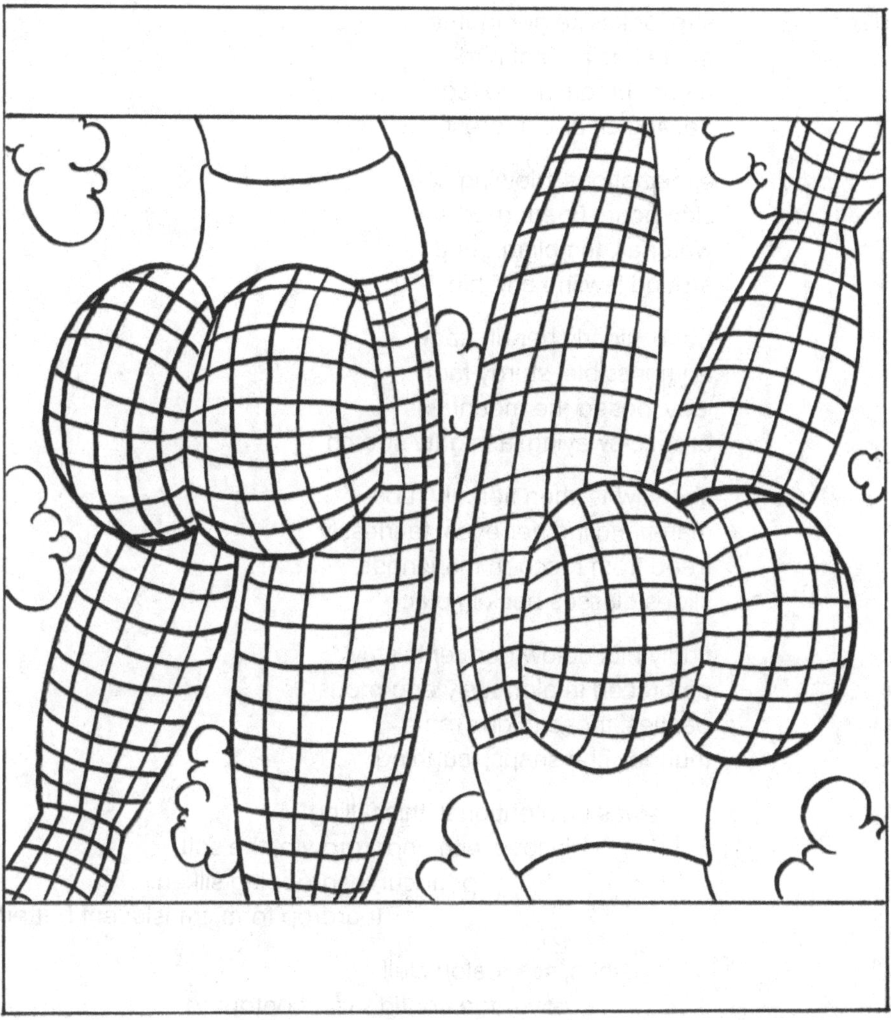

More Myself

with summer dancing off
storefront glass, a goddess
catches the light, twists
into molten lava legend

she looks like her mother
made her, radiant bird
nature blooming up legs
defying clear-cut forest

expectations. glowing
skin pours unadorned—
waterfall, tumbling gently
around jawline and hip

bone. clearly her rib cage
is impossible, sturdy farm
lady loosed the mountains
breeze-swaying. a mighty stretch

she yawns, then fiercely rubs—
man-handling her eyes, fearlessly
freed from raccoon markings
slides glasses back in place

fiddly bits below garments stay
embraced in gloriously enormous
panties. those thighs romp
thunder. she snaps, laughing

it was unintentional, this falling
in love with undergrowth, the soft
pear curve, drooping silken
teardrop form, translucent butterfly

brushes, scandalous full
coverage confidence, contoured
baby tree trunks, the whimsy
of flexibility—*my own shape*

This is a multidimensional wormhole, and you have no choice but to turn to page 85.

each night
spooning

Meet-Cute

I don't remember at all
how we met

perhaps you glimpsed me
and, smitten, swiftly bent

mock demure gesture
reverencing your queen—

but no, you were picking up
spilled hanky from bulging

khaki cargo shorts,
angling your generous noggin

so I could gaze, enraptured,
hair bleached so blond

or was it just frosted? tips
definitely gelled, either way

a full-bodied acoustic guitar leapt
into your charming piano-knuckled hands

all the young Christian women clutched
their ovaries and I prayed

not to fall victim
to a hopeless crush

trampled by ladies
drawn to your children's education

intention and discipleship Crest-sparkle
smile, toying with majors

like so many clambering women—
but not me, I would

expunge the memory of our meeting,
no credence given to your significance

for you surely won't last
beyond a footnote

my story destined for cuter
meets and less popular attractions

twenty years later
and I still can't unscramble

the jumble I made
of our first eye-clasp

the absence of this memory
will forever haunt me

Fear Flinging Romance

she slaps her belly
onto baseball field mud
sliding, all romance
á la Anne of Green Gables,
Jo March, and Fanny Price—
queen of observation
she embraces emotional nuances
magnifying each speck

heart hits the ground
next to his, rain-marinated
fingers slipping from hers—
is he Blythe, Teddy, or Edmund?
please not that rake, Crawford
he pulls her up. she wishes
the dark to hide her hope
newborn and easily startled

but he's there again pressing
muddy digits into her palm
this time he says to yell:
worst fear! fling it from your lips!
she hates to lie
but this truth is too scary:
she sees herself dying alone
an old lady never kissed
especially not by *this* beautiful boy

I long to lean back
through the decades
whisper past her fear
just one real unbelievable
future fact, wild as nature
surreal as great literature:
he is the best of them all
rolled into this man asleep
snug around my back

but if you go too soon

I have made space for you

s o   m u c h   s p a c e

each night spooning
the perimeter deeper
scooping away more
nonessential me

carefully contoured
my jigsaw-heart
to your shape
we slide so simply
in place, like kismet
the ease of flawless
triple axles, appearing
effortless despite
constant Kondo-ing
keeping all the best
of me, donating excess
(joyful self-farewells
make room for you)

there is nospace
between us
this is Love

but if you go too soon
how long will your form l i n g e r
g a p i n g   my soul
vacant?   your space
a V A C U U M roaring

Exhalation

—for Boz, again

weight of beauty, pink
champagne skyscraper settles
my chest pressed
exit for Burnside
vision of 2000s

I swear this air holds memory
the crush of hope
splits atoms
lodges in molecules
lingers like rose lure
drawing hilltop crowds

each dusk we return
sink into cupcake swears
Mission Theater musk
a Ram caught on 23rd
between crepes and confession

I wish that near-climax
burden—the atmosphere
your lips light as sunset

remember this tension

pull tight through each curve
looking for parking
wander Pioneer Square
breath so hungry
we see the proof
our sky tethered with us
bridging this frozen exhalation
echoing momentary eternity

our *Almost* sighs
caught over rosy city
until the world

e x p l o d e s

To take a deep dive into this love story, step out of this book-reading multiverse, go to joannrenee.com, and order *breath so hungry* (The Poetry Box, 2022).

If you wonder what can be created when two people love each other *very much* and aren't using birth control, go to page 97.

To split atoms and crawl inside of a pandemic home with three small children, go to page 125.

If you'd like to cross over to a slightly more peculiar multiverse and read some unusual love poetry, go to page 133.

one ocean, in a touch

Daddy

your strength is masked
towering evergreen in fog
you fade, observe—

        quiet witness
you owl the night
keep watch

elementary teacher mostly
summer security side gigs
cushion your saplings, cover
our growing grocery bill (plus
bonus: walks to Dairy Queen
split a Blizzard, keep commemorative
Clyde Drexler glass)

back home, lace fingers atop
your shining dome, daytime slumber
circulation ceases—
                thumbs empurple
idling motorcycle snores
overpower your window AC

Sundays you teach me to love
strolling together to church
this sacred tradition shared now
my own saplings walk
        our ambling path
                celebrate nature's pace

        roots steady
whispering branches—

you speak
        when ready

share your observations
and slide back into scenery

ex'cla•ma'tion!

—for Mama

meant for casual use
you spritz sparingly
only on Sundays
and special occasions—
chunky bottle
black and white
hot pink lettering
simple sweet
first morning scent
wafts upstairs.
vintage curling iron
burning hair
smoke-singed smell
mingles irreverently.
my still damp hair
fruity slick braids
Mama's fingers
woven deep
my scalp, your playground
underneath is mine
each tug a rope
we skip
rhythm connected—
we aren't the same—
I pull tighter
to feel her hands.
satin pillowcase
seams falling out
same since childhood
identical to hers—

rub the luxury
between index and middle.
incant old hymns
wake slow
nostrils flared—
hope for peach
apricot, amber
sandalwood Sunday

hope for her
downstairs
humming harmonies
wearing heavenly
wow!

I Should Probably Hug My Mama More

you b e c a m e first
inside of me. rich satin textures
sewn in my flesh. irresistible
features embrace you:
limitless bladder-trampoline
time, hot tub open 24/7
all you can eat cord-buffet

now, you complain
about cherry tomatoes, disturbed
by their pop, messy squirt
chin-dribble. you beg for more
screen time and outings. decide
what you want. s e p a r a t e—
but *I built you* in my tummy

and when our skin
c o n n e c t s—
palm on palm
cheek on knee
lips on forehead
shoulder on ear
arm on thigh—
we remember
without realization—
our breath slows
hearts steady
blood simmers low—
like cocooning
under a dozen heirloom
quilts, rain rivering through
eaves above, creating waterfalls
around our cozy nest:

this home we share
of skin and blood
DNA coursing back—
one ocean, in a touch

September: 1982

how can I write about being
born? that *has* to be the highlight
right? existence itself
takes the cake

sure, there was the year I turned
five, red teddy bear dress, high
pony, first Care Bear
height of bliss

and years eight and nine, basement
floor picnic, pigs 'n tiny blankets
jade Jell-o, fruit suspended inside
sublime

another year, early teen extravagance
six friends swimming at the Y, Papa
Aldo's. or my sixteenth, in all of its acne
and anticlimactic glory

twenty-one was sweet, pretending
to like my first martini, brie and pears
with my big sister, all my other friends
still illegal

or my all-inclusive megachurch swing
dance twenty-fifth, stir the pot
watch the drama, chocolate Costco yum
polka-dot swirling

maybe twenty-seven, first boyfriend blues
he sends embellished plum scarf from China
wrap myself in Sleeping at Last, then Doug Fir
Sondre Lerche kismet

golden thirty, preemie snuggles and fondue
too secluded, California haze. three years later
return to fall and Pacific Northwest
pumpkin patch cozy

I think thirty-five with all five final Boswells
pumpkin patch tromp, billowing charcoal drive
Grand Lodge nap, soak, tater tot, stout
well-played, transcendence

If you'd like to remember how this whole "Boswell" thing started, go to page 35.
To skip ahead approximately three light years, go to page 97.
If you would like to play a game of BINGO, go to page 201.

spaghettification

A Study in Sprouts

split trunks still grow
knotty protective skin
          hides trauma
in blatant daylight

I read reactions
in each generation:
burning bras
          buttoning up
reject, embrace, reject
technology,   shift again

home for months—
how is this shaping
you? future artists
dreamers, leaders
influencers;   my children

this bark scar, so low
foundational. how
          will you adapt?

where will you bulk up, stockpile strength?
aware already
          such dangers are
sneaks, now etched
in your tiny bodies
persistent as daisies

your arborist watches
in abject terror
hidden under smiles—

                    if I fail
          how will you twist?

Remote Learning

tiny-me stands
inside my brain
among the swirling neon seaweed synapses

little-me is trying
to fill the gaps
that big-me has forgotten / is forgetting

she is holding on
tying knots she hopes
are strong as sailor's, wishing she'd learned to sail

waiting with crossed legs
leaning against a sneeze
kids zoom past handing wee-me more threads

they flop and laugh
spinning *look at this!*
and *doesn't Mama look funny all twisted like that?*

tiny-me headstands
inside my mind
among the choking neon seaweed synapses

she's trying not to wink
out, a burst of too much
shattering the delicate tension of all the details she's sustaining

Sucks

I woke to a black hole
on my right temple
sucking me in
one atom   at a time

can one apply pressure
to the absence of matter
without getting slurped
into infinity-self?

like a loop of me
my arm circled through my brain
and back around, becoming still
my always right arm?

medicating this natural wonder
this cosmic pain
this aural migraine
dulls my senses

but I know she's still there
swirling nebulae underneath peppermint oil
blood thinners and CBD gummies
holed up, waiting for a break

in the storm. and we will rise
for she is me, and together, we
will make the kids breakfast
then teach math and science

we'll experiment on each other
learn what wipes the other out
our frenemyship might be a white dwarf
triggered into runaway nuclear fusion

supernova or not
we're back at the beginning again
too much matter has been squeezed
and you'll never see my spaghettification

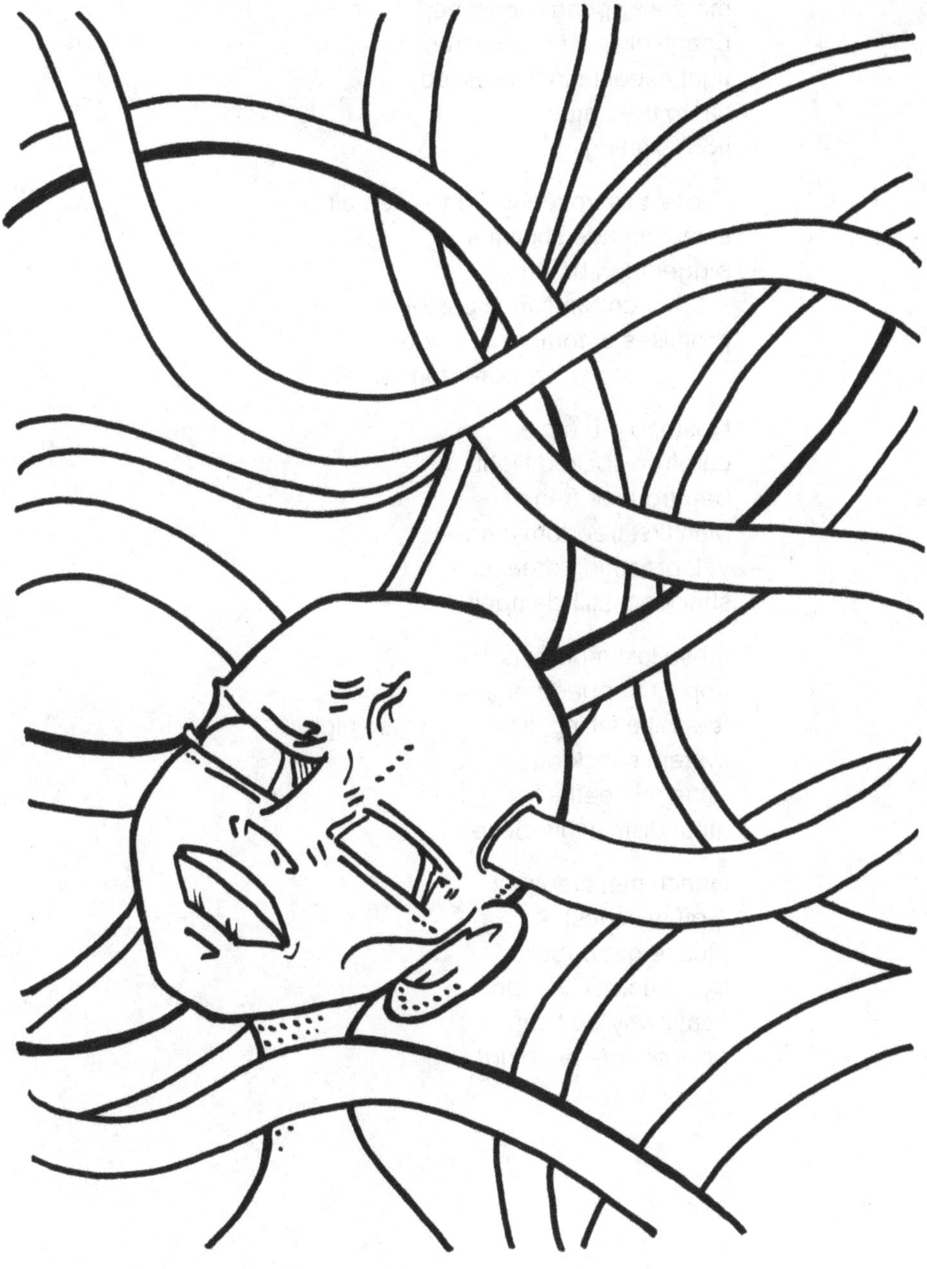

Coiled

I am t w i s t e d
mattress springs squashed
beautiful *b-o-i-n-g* repressed
tight expectations pressed
flat to the battered
IKEA slatting

above this frozen weight—I see air
sweet mirage shimmer
bigger than bright
          cotton candy pastel
promises of tomorrow's swell
                    roof-raising release

I taste b o u n c e
carefree socked flight
bed trounce trance
plan first freedom ping—
yet, breathing dreams
shackled, still clamped

these last moments
hope's trapped neighbor
feels like falling, from   so high
system shock buzz
rattle my teeth—
most dismal this close

launch me, elephant
—off my chest—
please get bubbly
like drunken Dumbo
float away, so I can
boi—oi—oi—oi—oing!

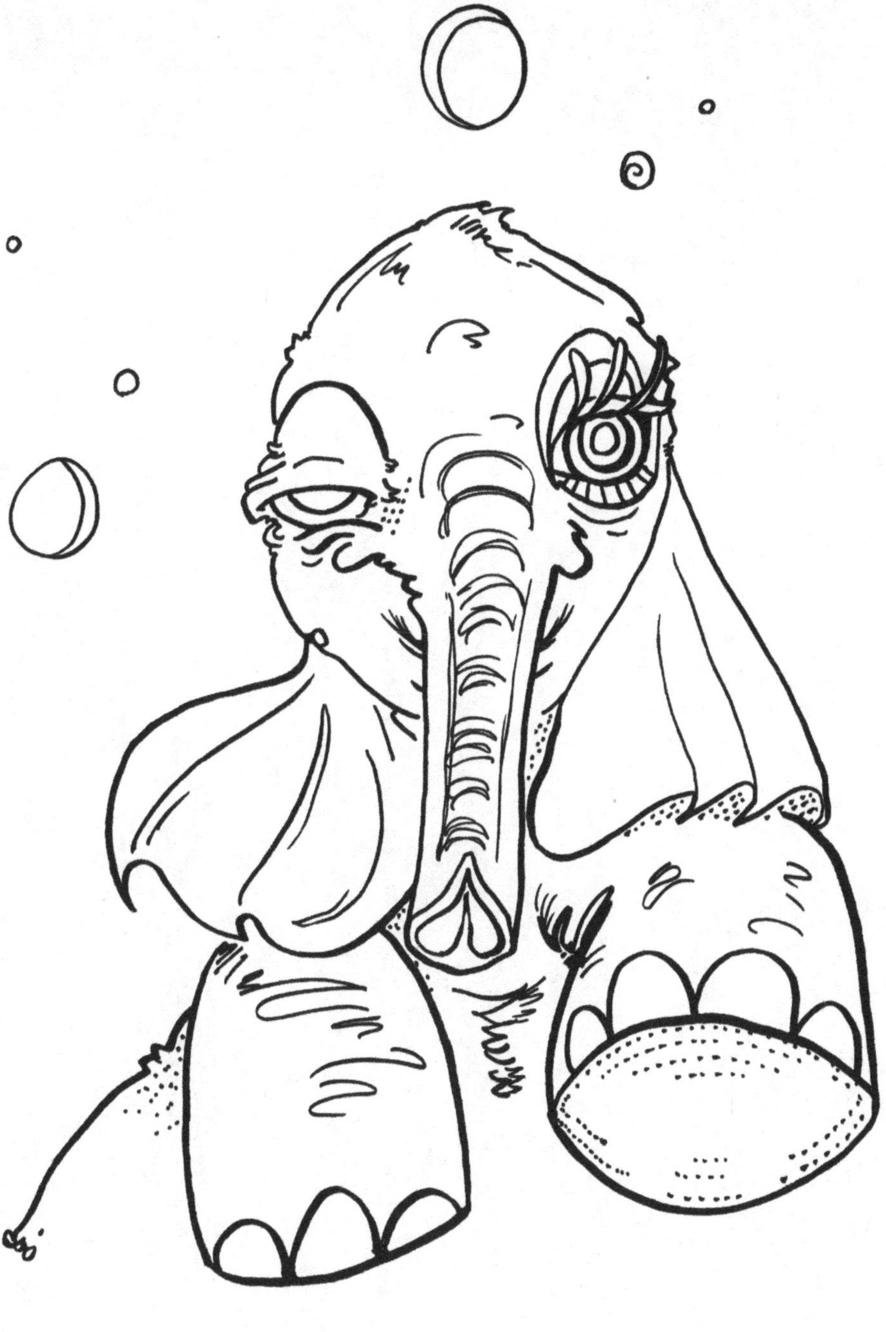

To skip past this uncomfortable deep space limbo, go to page 123.
If this drunken Dumbo has you feeling a little bit deliriously giddy, go to page 133.
Wow, this introspection is making you want to stare out of some windows. Go to page 191.

mending is my undertow

Jason

woke with a c r a c k e d heel
hard dry edges like the Grand Canyon
no blood, just tender abyss
like last week's jelly-filled donut
throbbing with attention
        apply ointment and bandage
tip-toe around—

paid for a man to be warm today
eleven dollars, Starlight Diner
where they serve
breakfast with kindness
        they let me stay
he said, *all day*

brief wide-eyed pause:
you have no idea
how hard it is to find someone
                        n i c e
after an hour imploring
ignored, turned down, even spat on
SUV speeding away—
just for asking, he said

no one expected this cold
        shelters won't open
till November. we hallucinate
together, sucked into winter's ventricle
prematurely, rub our fingers
seeking connection
an era before ATMs
        and cash-back limits

we pre-pay-day problem solve—
the hoops we leap to find humanity
I'm left, cracked further
heart chasm too big to Band-Aid

Tenant, noun: Stuck

> *Wasps feed their larvae with insects. An egg is laid on a paralyzed insect in the (chime) tube and a partition is built, then another egg room with an insect and so on until the wasp is done laying eggs or the tube is full.*

the wasps have a system
coordinated summer dance

they pretend ownership so long
we give them the deed

now they charge
aggressive landlords on stolen ground

I am a paralyzed cricket
waiting to be sucked dry

such pale green, I thrum
inside another's haven

even pandemic won't help, housing
prices climb eleven percent

before the sting, my partner flourished
running debt-free, family property

his grandmother's chimes hang
above our rented deck

a bit of dead straw and my hair
poke up, nearly comic, this tragedy

our stridulation gongs within
these conical heirlooms

dizzy-busy buzz—
will predatory lenders miss us?

our credit is on the line
bleaching in sunlight

we've slipped through tubing
stunned survival
spared
from the culling

nocturnal, we rise
pardoned apocalyptic tide

you'll find us
bathing in moonlight

zip through Zillow listings, crave
grass and stars, our own unfenced yard

bank bullies harbor stingers
we pay and pay, waiting

for an impossible drop:
an affordable slice even for dreamers and poets

Bon Iver

when I can't get up
sunken mattress barge
all afloat on emotion
mending is my undertow

deep melancholy
buried in each bone
saturated into broth—
ennui-enriched body

I imagine water
seek a good ship
je vousdrais entendre
*Bon Iver tous les jours**

there's art in this storm
at my holocene center
where moods rock me
a child deep in chicken noodle

I am my own
winter boat
fog leaks light
at the horizon

this mood is soup
setting sail at icy dawn
so many miles
before brisk dusk

sink teeth into frosted veins
savory healing
be my own mother
les miserable milk immersion

gothic myth, I bob
unmoored, unhindered, unapologetic
waves crash as they will
uneven meter beats beauty into chaos

* French: I would like to hear Bon Iver every day.
Bon Iver is a band. The name means "good winter" in French.

Luminous Loosening

thread keeps snapping
tension set too tight

bobbin jammed
balling up knots

double thick Coats & Clark cotton
juts up, sprouting through feed dog

Mama says start over
rethread the whole machine

Mama says a lot of things
but this thought is a foot pedal, l a u n c h i n g beyond her intent

needle leaps through fabric walls
a million times, perforates perfection

I balance my now
with expected outcome

there's comfort in this
twisty-back quilt

one hand holds lemon loaf
tea, an acceptance of alternate wonderful

the other is wrapped in final product
blissed out with frustration jumbles

thumb my imperfections
and replay the release

let *this* be different
than planned

such serene satisfaction in process
squeezing time through presser foot

I am trying out the luminous
lost in mystical calico hum

To launch into a world where things aren't as they should be, go to page 145.
If you'd like to explore a space filled with frustrations, go to page 181.
If you'd like to get lost even more in some mystical *boom-ba-room*, go to page 243.

impossible things

Diagnosis

two Joanns in the waiting room: a dark gag

the constant name calling
confusion deepens concern—
is her outlook better than mine
or grimmer?

a terminal disease
quick to the punch?
or this slow burn
slowly stripping a decade from life?

expectancy is tricky
the hyper-hope tumble—
behold weeping lobby displays
rolling IV drip thrones

each tragic deity holds a card
in that magic bracelet—
can we swap them?
take my chances with an unknown

could it be Covid?
cancer? conjunctivitis?
centrifuges spin too quickly
for me to grow thicker skin

even with glasses
d i s t a n c e   is brutal
at six feet   you blur
blank-faced ER blobs

is that a smile?
a wink? a wince?
staff is gentle but firm—
I may not trade my disease for hers

my body is a wonder
land heavily booby
trapped, each step
uncertain and tender

these doctors say impossible things

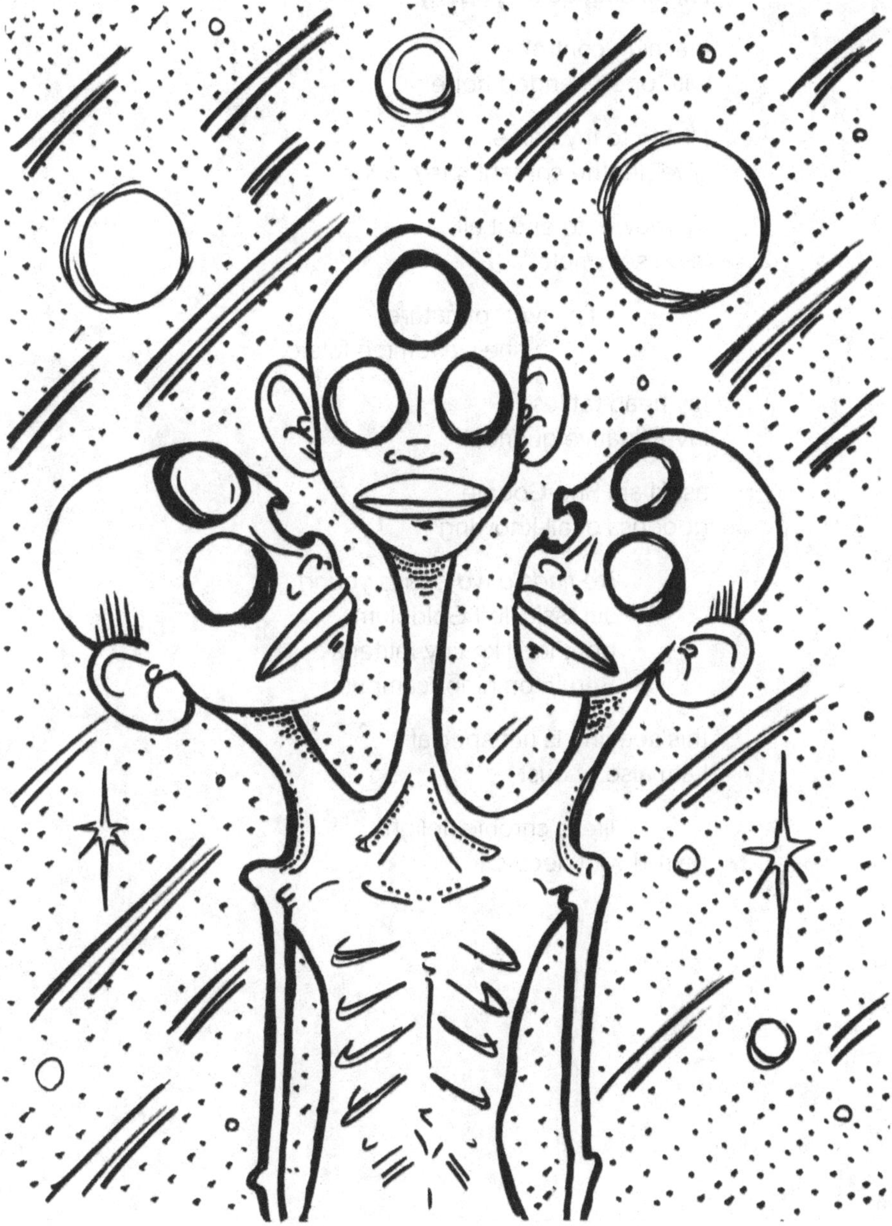

The Natural Chaos of All Living Things

can you feel this tension
I'm holding quite gingerly?

leashing control
with open-handed hope

I listen to my frame
give her the content she craves

the power to end it all
is oh so simple

a tiny twist of nature
she's a femme fatale

my head rattles
investigative queries

as if I am She-Google
goddess of all-knowing

life finds a way, says young
Jurassic Jeff Goldblum
perched like tiny-mittens-
Bernie on hippocampus

this seeking is not special
I am also of dust

life *is* chronic delight
paired with decay:

the cousin who loved
animals and art, but then: leukemia

the harpist and chaplain
bearing arthritis so soon

the coastal Doug Fir reaching
for sunlight, bending to survive

gravity compels me to root
in Earth's chaotic journey

this is *my* harrowing
story: organized artist

waving farewell to just
one mere fragment of existence

when is an eddy a whirlpool?
when is it a maelstrom?*

my power is slipping
but this skin is still waterproof

* stolen from a January 2021 Beth Woolsey blog post

Vitamin String Quartet

watch the dead branches dance today
see how the wind tricks each brittle twig, lifted
high from treacherous limb, dangling percussion—
my hair, too, can't die out here in pretend spring

I lean into escape, open this coat
Earth is breathing, I need her lungs
between my breasts *thump-thump-thump*
regency scintillation brush my wrist's belly

soft this moss on stone pulse
won't be defined by decay, downpour
vibrato vitamin surges, I surf
waves of well-being—my lovely, I go

deep dive scandal daydream indulgences—
sweets off limits, my body and brain
wake winter's debris within
risk every element, rustle some life

To follow scintillation's blush and play some strip poetry, go to page 27.
If you'd like to rustle some life into this cold planet, go to page 67.
Okay, that was too deep into a very personal orbit. Find out where everyone went by going to page 133.

fork ourselves
a feast

Simmery Sexy Summer

it's gonna be a real-ass scorching summer
ladies licking upper lip sweat-salt summer
bikini c-section scar flaunting summer
beached body flowing relaxed summer
ghost tummy jean skirt / crop top summer
so wet hot swampy drawers summer
sunscreen slather slip-n-slide summer
sloshy post-pandemic vaxxed party summer
neighbors screaming "who-let-the-dogs-out?" summer
new BBQ, who is this? summer
rainbows roaring super lit 2021 summer
dragon onesie sunset makeout summer
no damn time to tame this summer
we're gonna fork ourselves a feast of marmalade summer

Summer Crush

I am falling hard
for my legs this summer

when I cross them
in shorts, they blossom

sink my fingertips in supple
inner thigh, tender memory

then around to outer muscle bounce
resistant to deeper probing

they're so sturdy
down to sensitive kneecap nerve

when I kneel, I must
be tender

whisper sweet
nothings so gentle

and still they swagger
dancing sister limbs

they are so strong
and hairy

and approximately the size
of small tree trunks

which march like Ents
through forests, these friends

inseparable chopsticks
kicking to the beat, fighting the heat

they never tan
nor burn

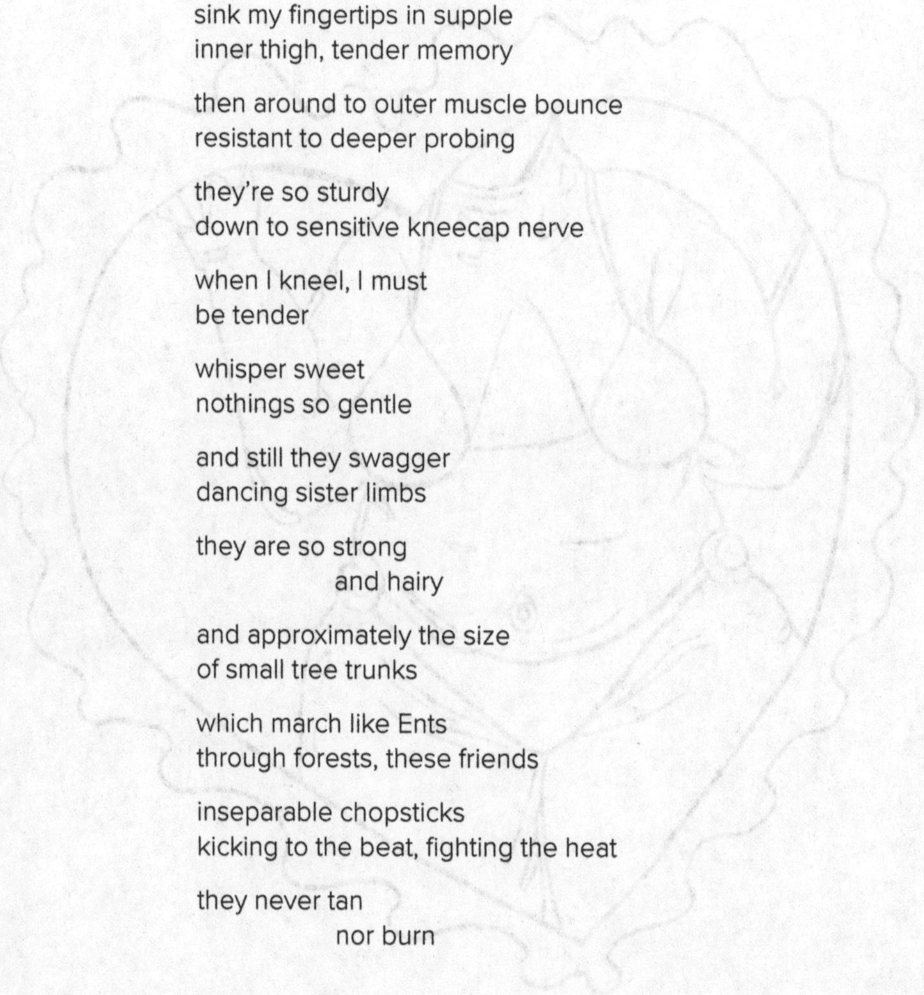

such beautiful silvery squiggle
stretch marks by my knees

and little purpley veins
and tiny crimson specks

and more than a few freckle
constellations, such dreams we trace

recall the journeys
they've graced me

predict the paths
yet to emerge

Spun Silver

took my tummy out
to the farmers market
for a sack of Oregon peaches
and two engorged Washington zucchini

she is sugar
spun silver threading
contrail reminders of pregnancy
zigzag belly bliss

despite swimming babies inside
she was virginal, always hidden
a secret too sacred to be shared
with strangers' eyes and wandering minds

at thirty-eight I am freeing her:
bought a scandalous forest
green crop top and now the world
may watch her wiggle

she is cream
churning butter maiden
each step sways around her backbone core
and my children are mesmerized

hypnotizing warrior queen
commands attention
and I apologize for every second
I was ashamed of her dimply radiance

Birdy Bits

And the Bird become flesh and dwelt among us
and we have seen their glory.
—Joann 1:14 (a play on John 1:14)

feel them flex—put you under
their hex, this complex flesh

they can wiggle
they can swagger

so near the twin fire-swamps
my smoldering pits

sprout dangly bits
meat wings

strong enough to unfurl
a full span of skin and bone

they can flap
they can follow through

when squeezed to my sides
they flatten like paper

they can fold up
these magical origami cranes

all this space to admire
spaghetti strap summers

so quickly they speckle
with natural daylight graffiti

they can reach
to the tippy-top bunk

my children try to connect
the little brown dots with their fingers

bouncing studiously up past the funny bone
then ask quietly if I'm offended

I giggle with pride, show them
our secrets—what else we can do:

we can slice water
pull our full glorious weight through

we can wield a racket
return wild balls with a screech

we can love each formal wear photograph
no wraps or tiny black glitter cardigans

just these soaring uncaged arms
divine fleshy functionality

Butt, I Love You Too

waxing gibbous meets waning gibbous

two moons twin	a broken locket
joined by crevice	forever gently grazing
friends who hold	space for farts
a sigh of dimples	spray each cheek
perky potholes	map their landscape
together traverse	the world, jolly sags
fill cotton briefs	stretch grateful
jeggings, they take	turns at forward
strides, flattening	before the left behind
bulge, both movements	a triumph of motion
but oh the curve	as caboose seeks rest!
they become one	luscious peach
posterior, perfectly	squished tush cushion
seated rear spreads	into ripe-ass sofa
a lounge for the whole	body on this booty
musical chairs pull this	derrière twerk-ward
friend, she has no true	skill for those wicked wiggles
but	she's not bummed out

This body seems amazing! To explore what's going on below the surface, go to page 77.

If you noticed that this poem can be read both across the crack as well as down each individual cheek, go to page 171 to read about the poet who made that suggestion.

If you've stared too long at the human body and would now enjoy a good stare out of a portal window, go to page 191.

after macaroni we drive

Four and a Half

—for Teddy

I must paint the soft
rosy expanse of your cheek

my kisses unrestrained: *it's nice to meet you*
lips so quickly acquainted with this canvas

your face, so little—so full
of words and nighttime wonderings

Mama, I think your name is
also Mommy. Mmm! I love you, Cute!

I think your name is Cute—my *Cute—*
are the monsters on the moon?

you call me your baby
arms tightening around my neck

flattening my left ear
against your pitter-pat heart

I listen, hypnotized
and follow your instructions

calling you *Mama* makes you
giggle-grin, puff out your pajama'd chest

you achieve the impossible
each night charming

me further, under your spell
I stay longer than I mean to

whispering back your catch phrase:
It's good everywhere

Highway 101

—also for Teddy

hold my body rigid
          a tightrope
as if I could climb
out of my skin, flipping
contortionist into your backseat belly
use my own breath
magic elixir to ease
each discomfort—
my circus act is *Mother*

but I've held too taut
          this tension settles
no tummies, only parades
clown cars into my temples
they tumble down my spine
perform prat falls—
my lower back a trampoline
and still my child is not amused
their stomach succumbs to acrobatic beach
highway twists too big for the big top

Open Universe

—for Clara

when you split your forehead
like a womb, I pop
the bite-sized Milky Way between your lips
gather a warm crimson cloth, gently
caress your open universe
c r a c k e d now
with *w h y ? ! ?*

after macaroni we drive through dusk, discuss
what to expect as you face this new truth
I wrap you in summer's picnic quilt and hope
not vacant of reality
you talk of cutting bangs, keeping them long
while you make threats—this will *n e v e r*
enter the pages of your journal

at the hospital you lock the car door
then defeated walk the sky bridge
turn your eyes away from nighttime's hallway
make friends instead with each new-baby visitor
shiver until your turn for glue and butterfly wings
relief at "no stitches" eclipses wishes for bed—
now you hunger for milkshake

the next morning I shroud
each mirror with pillowcases
invite you to peer between the fibers
when you are ready, welcome
fresh adventure itching like the cosmos
mending its way into your brow

Monthly

—also for Clara

you scraped your toe
kept right on running until
you spied your blood, crumpled
like some of your art
you think isn't good

you sob, honestly
terrified you won't be allowed
a n y w h e r e
especially not wizard school—
disqualified for bleeding

you ask me if you can still go
if they will know and point
if you will ever smile
a g a i n

I look around slowly
like the couch is our tree
house, no boys allowed
(though perhaps they should
know too)—lean in

twinkle-whisper,
I'm bleeding right now!
and I went swimming
and bought groceries
and danced in the kitchen

I made you pancakes
and wrote a poem
and snuggled with Daddy—
all while releasing my red

where?! you breathe awed, horrified
scan me for signs of injury
from my vagina! I beam
pride in my power, look at me!
I can bleed for *days*!

you pause—
            I think you are teasing me
incredulous eyes test mine
look at my pants, *I don't see anything*

I catch it in a cup, a royal goblet!
remember, I say, *blood is our strength*
someday you will join me!
we'll bleed in stealth or right out loud
we'll be friends with our bodies
                        understand our power!

you have no response for this
right now, that's okay—
go learn Quidditch, my dear
your toe has already healed

You are riveted. And hungry. Grab a snack and then continue to the next page.

managing the mush

In a Twist

girls: dainty, feminine
p e r f e c t
all sugar and spice

boys: rugged, masculine
b r a v e
all mischief and dirt

these tropes I *know*
s e x i s t
all bias and fluff

persistent they trickle
like water torture
one drip after another

insistent on binaries
boring holes with: dolls
for girls, trucks for boys

makeup for girls, camo for boys
smiles from girls, strength from boys
calm from girls, while boys will be boys

with each drop, marketing enforces:
b e a u t y for females
p r a c t i c a l i t y for males

—and I bought the panties
my preschool daughters would wear
unaware how deep these sexist layers go

until my third-born, a son
began training, his underwear sturdy
absorbent they declare, *accidents happen!*

he can tinkle a teeny
without creating puddles
they gird him in comfort

secure, he runs
they won't slip
when he does

so soft and full
he knows no wedgie—
embraced completely

now I'm enraged—
this is how *all* butts
should be treated

when my girls were taught control
the tiniest leak
trickled sticky leg rivulets

each dribble, public
embarrassment. reminder:
there is no space for mistakes

shame still hot
clean panties pucker in back
while sliding down slender hips

thicker knickers aren't for girls
sexy cuts revealing cheeks
and delicate thin waistbands abound

even for young girls, who grow
concerned about panty lines
and periods, then become mothers

spilling with sneezes, oozing
mid-monthly ovulation, *still*
choose impractical coverage

while our male counterparts
drip into their drawers
if they don't shake enough

I didn't know there could be
a better way, and now
I'm pissed

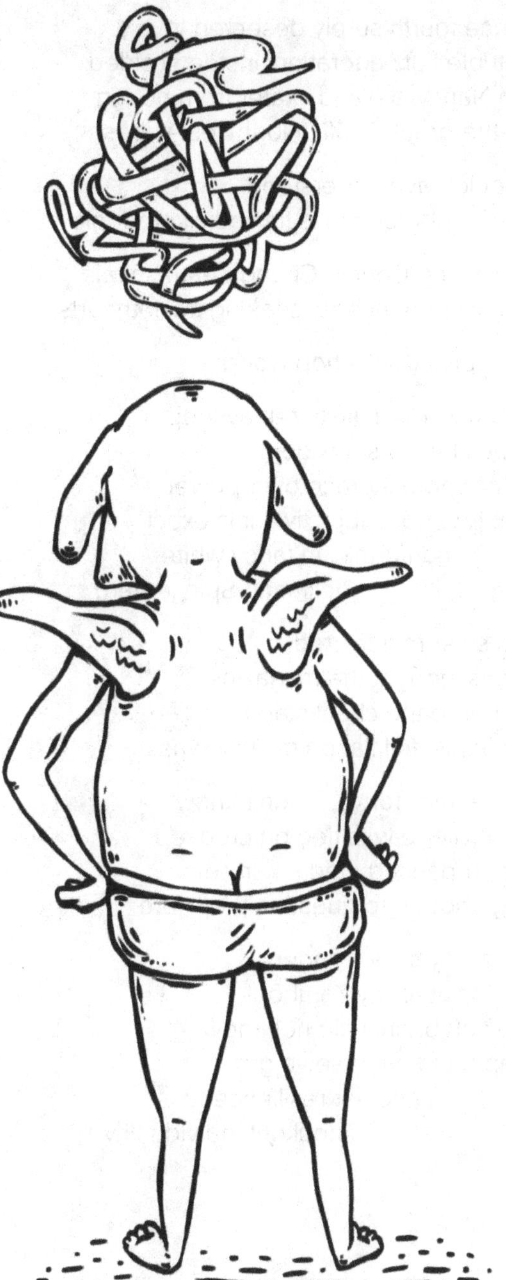

My Apology to Tonya Harding

France fourth surely deserved love
tall triple Lutz adoration, instead I sided
with Nancy, a bland skater from boring-
not-the-great-Pacific-Northwest-is-best

I should have understood
perception is flawed, like people

sure, when Connie Chung death spirals
I'm sucker punched, seeking sweethearts

good girls don't chop wood

convinced by infinity replay loop
judges binary set is gold:
I must choose grace over power
beauty is not subjective, it is exact
conformity in fancy white
Biellmann Spin leotard

I am so sorry I trusted
biases, bought the magazine
devoured the checkstand
highlights, fell flat on my naive ass

forgive me, Tonya, I didn't know
my privilege was tied on crooked
I never paused media's sit spin
long enough to question the score

patriarchy's thick fingers
manipulated my Zamboni-
free soft brain. I did not know
to applaud hand-sewn grit
concealer resilience
knockout individuality

I snuggled you up with OJ
pairs skating through my head
duo of ill-intent, guilty guilty guilty
my heart beat for Kristi, ashamed
the notoriety you Salchowed into my home
state. I didn't even know solid landing
triple Axel pride belongs to you—
Minneapolis and Munich 1991 glory

what hard-hitting journalism overpowered
your edgy skating superpower, twisting
American class drama like laces
delighting when they snap mid-routine?

you should have been my hero—
butt-kicking bow and arrow badass
record-breaking Oregonian goddess

Gross Negligence

yes, the orphans
with their suds and rags
and belted vocals, leaping
from cots. yes to dangling off fire
escapes. yes to their toe
stomping attempts for love

but after this shuttered year
squished inside with *lit-tle*
girl, lit-tle girl, lit-tle one—
their needs echoing down halls
building a hive in my brain—
I found forgiveness and a yes

for Miss Agatha Hannigan
managing the mush, her lonely
heart, and the desperation of dozens
of tiny loud people trapped indoors
and she is alone with her paycheck
of bathtub gin and dirty radio romance

sure, she could've been kinder
kissed and comforted
instead of threatening and teasing—
but where were the resources
the people, the spirited support
of any-damn-body for more than Annie?

Miss H *stayed*, that lost-causes-soul
buried below miles of government neglect
and when it really mattered
the mama-bear came out, bet her final shimmy
and battled her brother, determined to pull
that crimson sunshine out of harm's way

and tomorrow? she rides out, a queen
draped over elephant—the party
swirls around her, pardon like pearls
lights her up. she looks like me—
finally cared for, she can care
again, and I will love her eternally

Mothers Always

have love for all—
fierce bear snuggles
snarls for predators
          we can fight
while kissing boo-boos

we're a sisterhood—
welcome to the club!
of course we have rules:

acceptable mothers
are apolitical
        asexual
and of course
                (a)Christian
          or maybe (a)Catholic
     that one's okay too
we guess

you won't notice
us sharing memes
except of cute pets
and adorable children

our Insta stories are full
of the days' debris:
snack time, first steps
French braids, train tracks
finger paints, fast asleep

we could cry all day
watching Southern children
sing praise songs on YouTube
          share to Facebook
tag twenty friends

let's weep in unity
          this is our code
what brings us together:
life's miraculous balance
beauty and fragility

this sacred calling
won't be besmirched
with any calls to action
by dying Black men*
pressed onto concrete
claiming our tribe*

our tears are also
not for the babies at the border
sleeping on concrete
no way to find Mama

we aren't for them
but we're not *against* them—
we're merely separate from them
it's not our place
to help by speaking up

we empathize
really, we do
so maybe a vague verse
posted for all sides
to like, thumbs up all around!

we could get into dress code
and approved exclamations
for frustrating moments *(egads!*
brussels sprouts! fiddlesticks!)
but I think you get the point:
try not to offend anyone
that's the golden rule of motherhood

to receive your sorority pin
simply burn your jeggings
and change your FB identity
to include your husband's* name
(i.e. JohnJane Smith)

we look forward
to adding your voice to our collective

* In late May 2020, George Floyd was killed by police officers, and witness videos show that in between him saying that he couldn't breathe, he also called out for his mama.
* Tribe is language white Christian women use profusely, unable or unwilling to recognize the inappropriate cultural appropriation in using this term for themselves.
* There is a broad assumption that Christian mothers are married to men.

If you would prefer not to ignore the needs of those outside your immediate family circle, go to page 145.
If you wish adding your name to a collective wasn't quite so complicated, go to page 181.
To take a few moments for a guided Old Testament devotional, go to page 215.

Dead End

Oh heavens! You've collided with Loki in an insignificant nexus, and you've been split into two practically identical beings! You must each go your own way now.

If you are wearing sturdy, comfortable undies, go to page 47 (chapter 4).
If you are wearing something that merely hints at the idea of underwear, go to page 201 (chapter 18).

feet become
floorboards

Sacred Assembly

—for #704

we live   i s o l a t e d
mere feet   from   each   other
quiet but for stair running
and Caribbean keyboard
pounding at nap time—
the heartbeat of your teen
through our townhome wall

press palm—to—textured eggshell
feel Johnny Depp   p u l s e
spray of salt and sun
slap me silly, Zimmer melody
shimmy Davy Jones deep
share space-separated
                                        escape

I Just Want to Make Oatmeal. Can You Please Occupy Yourselves for Just Fifteen Minutes? All of You? Please?

so simple, the desire—
ripe strawberries afloat
warm oats, all at sea
almonds awaken sugar lips

so simple, the seed—
hungry mouth urgency
always need, fill the air
with cotton candy grape cravings

so simple, the need—
pillow fights release
roar, crowds roof cage
we tumble, blendered berries

so simple, the smoosh—
déjà vu coils weeks into another
Mama puddle grants sweet
treats to assuage demands

so simple, the home—
we melt into walls
feet become floorboards
frantic house sated with want

Casual Caking

we've taken to wetting the bed
licking the plates, marching for reform

we now pee in the garden
munching mint after

yard-less, our driveway is bistro
by night, amusement park by day

at the store, whizz past the produce
hit up that clearance bakery rack

between seafood and public restrooms
choose a seven-dollar chocolate sheet

we're leaning in to casual caking
sing Happy Birthday to no one

soon it'll be Charlie Brown Thanksgiving
feasts of popcorn and pretzels on the daily

wizards of the now, magic eats us
consuming and consumed: we are blowing cotton

see that toilet brush? if I leave it
under my pillow, will the fairies come?

what is tomorrow but a mirage
of vaccines and school openings?

we've taken to kicking the calendar
drinking from the pot, skinny-dipping in the shower

if we go outside, sing about our shot, step over dog shit
are we throwing our anxiety away?

HAPPY BIRTHDAY, NO ONE!

Cinnamon Pandemic Summer Spiral

are we here yet? / no? we ate the marshmallow / too fast. UN says / eat those wilting veggies. / methinks we have impulse / control issues. ask that dude, / is he Proud or Border / Patrol goon, swoopy / with Trix, no moms allowed. / neighbor wears Red, / Mama agrees the Silent Americans / should protest censorship, / but oh those BLM fa-natics / across the river! stop with the paint! / tear gas makes sense / to combat the free-dom-works / that are just fire beyond Independence / Day. time is the ultimate infection. / do we go to the woods, / or buy wood? or just lose it, / like Woody in Toy Story 4? / it's our fifthly moonth-adversity / and I'd like to get it right— / cause that exists still: / we can know things, / research inter webs, / hashtag Godvibes: / did you know there's facts? / provable as farts. / wooden Adam Driver spoon / the gift unto myself / nachosex vibes / hazy tuning fork vertigo now. / what phase is this? / follow the-yellow-brick-what? / past poppies and doggie poopies / the way shut is littered in fad waves, / licking at our toes, pickle popcorn fish: / bike walk, kick ball, loose teeth, / mug du jour, hammock, / hold me closer tiny humans, / kitty walk, Red Robin delivery, / march, double beach, new beds / garden pee, slowly deflating pool, / all Minecraft, umbrella deck party, / the floor is lava, driveway double dates, / poetry zoom, launch books like rocket duds, / dude won't pee, splash pad, / stop touching me little fries / home slice giant flies / still March / no, with feet / not the month still. or yes? / are we 21 yet? and if we are, / who shattered the champagne mirage I ate for breakfast? / this three shall pass / friends leap off build-ings / sheet-capes and Lycra / their invincibility complex / stupidity superpower / plunge into imaginary / herd immunity, still years off / if you can't abstinence / please still use protection / practice safe separation / masks are your best / condom friends. I imagine / thumb wars come November. / banjo picking brains / I'm not dizzy, / you're dizzy / go home inbox, you drunk / filthy full, can has petitions? / ass sweat pretty Rorschach seat / I trip body pool noodle / this time is just hammock / me baby pizza / rock-a-bye taco suntan / I frosting queen / full stop spiral / cinnabon sanity unwound. / eat me back-wards right meow / just read the red / hey, now I'm 100 lines if I wasn't loopy

---

If you are dizzy and that makes you wish for a parent, go to page 27.
If you are dizzy and that makes you have a headache, go to page 59.
If you have no idea what you just read and wish that the poet had kindly written this out in lines, go to page 155.

aliens will farm

Where Are They Now?

Mr. Tumnus is a Proud Boy
the White Witch blocked me on social
I hope Mr. Beaver is still composing
Aslan cares for the elderly
I'm still searching for Susan

one Algernon is Something Rotten
tours with Broadway
one Cecily (fancy woman) composes
solo and with Mr. Beaver
Benedict can still act, also, hair
stylist at a wigmaker's wedding

dropout Grandpa Lawrence is a rock star
Laurie went to Cornish
Marmie studies marine biology in Belgium
Jo is Interim Pastor Chastity Joy
Amy seems happy

Mayor Shin (talented never joiner)
there's no way of knowing
the Music Man himself is a new master
according to Mom's social

George Webb is crazy about Jesus
Christ and his wife
Mrs. Webb left her town, reigns
as Aries Mama and YMCA queen

Helena, Taproot pizza-loving advocate
Bottom, special education paraeducator
Quince, fluid Harlequin glory
Flute, just married, Hands-On reception
Lysander, soul explorer
Hermia, NYC dancer

the Modern Major General finished his mission
the Pirate King is La MaMa theater genius
and Mabel, barefoot in a tree for Edinburgh Fringe

my part was so little
cast as a minor role
in their glorious unspooling
live-action documentaries

I was support
storyteller, listener
advice-giver
teacher, producer
director

show posters line my garage stairway
stars stringing a constellation
billions of light years away
squint to make out memories
thousands of hours summed up
in eight-dollar flimsy frames

I don't know how to feel
but I do anyway

zip-up faded theater
hoodie, thunderbird looks
nostalgic. flip the lights
back off. close the door

Venus

you think it's hot here, surprised
that your physiology isn't supreme—
I'm shocked you frozen Neanderthals
even evolved enough to find us

        we didn't need your discovery
we flourish regardless, whizzing
around you, quite dramatic runaway tease
your star-crossed microbial mystery muse

you made Earth the norm for life, confused
when alien biosignatures are alien
I don't want to be rude, but, *duh*
open your exploratory instruments wider

such puny imagination—
        is it arrogance or ignorance?
poor things climbing into metal
to stroll through your clouds

and all that putrid sweet polluting
those gloriously natural scents
sniff our tantalizing primordial jungle
how cute your sulfur imitations

what you call rancid
diapers of Satan's spawn
        we call *Eau de Phosphine*
no goddess is complete without

Vile Venus, you reply
(we're merchandizing that one)
persistent, nasty possibility
        thirty miles up, you say

hellscape surface, inhospitable furnace—
astonishing you still can't reinvent life parameters
we are even now in your minds
yellow hazy greenhouse energy

        an estimated abundance
very final and macabre*

* based on “A Possible Sign Of Life Right Next Door To Earth, On Venus,” Nell Greenfieldboyce, NPR (https://www.npr.org/2020/09/14/912619891/a-possible-sign-of-life-right-next-door-to-earth-on-venus)

Superheroes of the Unwilling Womb

someday aliens will farm
me monthly for eggs

impeccable galactic charts will note
my desire *not* to grow anymore

children, and so they hover, invisible
precision transports commence the instant

they drop, before fertilization can occur
advanced beings swivel on orbiting bar stools

impatiently twirl antennae, tiny
mouths dictate breakfast desires

and cosmic cooks whip my matter
into frenzied scrambles while another primitive

earthling's nearly-offspring is boiled
or poached. unknowing below, we slumber

restful, trusting contraceptives or abstinence
superheroes of the unwilling womb

we wake emptied, roust the chicken coop
or fridged egg-crate, prepare them fried

over-medium. forks dripping golden
possibilities. never asking the hen

if rooster was around when she lay
delicious opal oval, or even for consent

Space Bar

you dirty little bookend
birthed of all
letters and symbols
h u m m i n g   down below

you incessant child
constant interrupter
but then you   s t u t t e r   silent
gap-maker, gaping me   s t a c c a t o

you sneaky elegant lover
I like to caress your   l e n g t h
smooth and glossy
where you let my thumbs rest

you precious Quaker mystic
i n s e r t i n g   yourself
beautiful white space
reminding me to   b r e a t h e

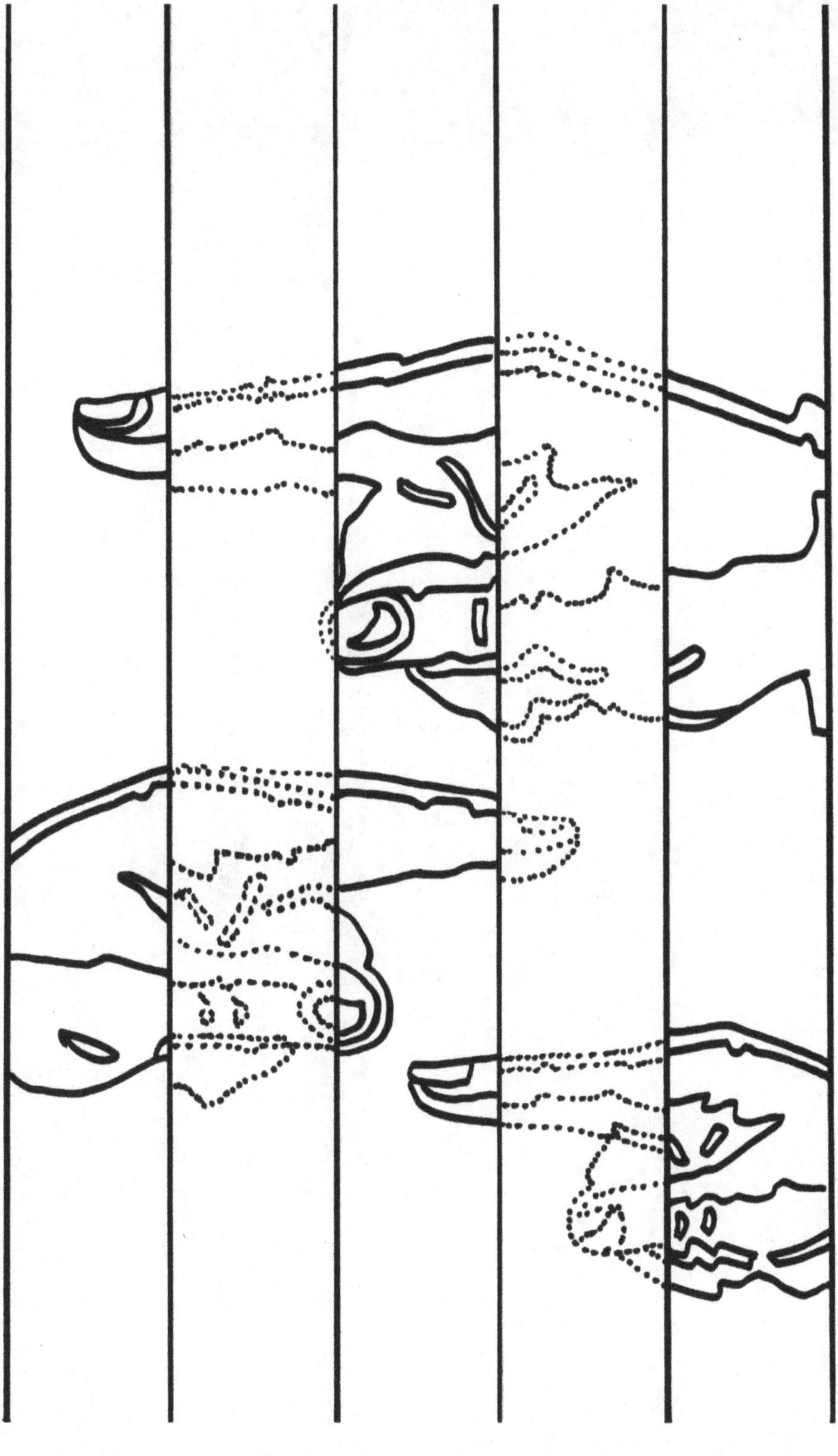

Autumnal Netflix & Chill

when I imagine a field of buttercups
it is a porcelain meadow of tiny
mugs billowing in the breeze
melted marigold enchanting interiors
golden sunshine bubbling merrily
awaiting autumn's imminent Popcorn Tree
clatter underfoot, just before salt hail
assails us all saline, then we slip
sail into hibernation harbor, prepare
to cast cozy, fingertips dripping magic

To cast yourself deep into a meta-verse of forest bathing, go to page 27.
If you wish to go to a world made entirely of buttered popcorn, go to page 123.
To take a cross-country journey in a suitcase, go to page 171.

compress
my rage

Deescalation

—for Jenoah Donald and Kevin Peterson Jr.

if I compress my rage
smaller and more dense
a glowing ball turns marble
beneath my breastbone
where I am holding quite still
visualizing the scene
only a mile from October
where they set up
then murdered
Kevin, just for selling
                    X a n a x

and now I'm yet more speechless
lips straight as a baton
outwardly restrained
all aquiver within—
        four deputies at a traffic stop

how can I break
a system so violent?

my poetry is nothing:
        a muted scream of agony
        a white housewife wailing
        a panic of pixels buried

if I compress my rage
impossibly dense
a glowing ball becomes marble—
a great collection now of marbles
        beneath my breastbone
        where I am held so still—
will this congregation of stone
become brilliant? Big Bang
burning us all new? another
chance in a long string of infinite
restarts. for what is left
to save us
        but our own spark?

protester / police

future dreams for those we pay to protect and serve

dress them in flowers
uniform of peace for police
these volunteers determined
to assuage the harm
systemically dumped
since dawn of time
by their precursors
powerful privilege bearers

protection posture
they kneel
bulletproof
but unarmed
hands up
don't shoot
deescalate
from weaker ground

guns changed
for tools that defuse:
white flags holstered
with patience, calm
Band-Aids, candy canes
empathy, understanding
giant ears, plus microphone for you
and oxygen tanks. so much oxygen

new costumes reflect
years of conflict training:
hearts sewn on sleeves
spill over rank markings
overshadowing stars, and
stripe reminders sprout
up pant legs:
serve with love

stations host potlucks
where honored guests
share sacred scarred stories
remembrances of brutality
their grandparents, parents
and children suffered/suffer
together they all put on
shrouds of mourning

sew more patches
promises more vigilant
than body cams
blue lives choose
this uniform graffiti
softening starch
join the march for justice
when one of their own

crosses the line *again*
it's slow
trust must be
re-earned
              and earned
for the first time
they are always open
to criticism. willing to learn

SERVE
WITH LOVE

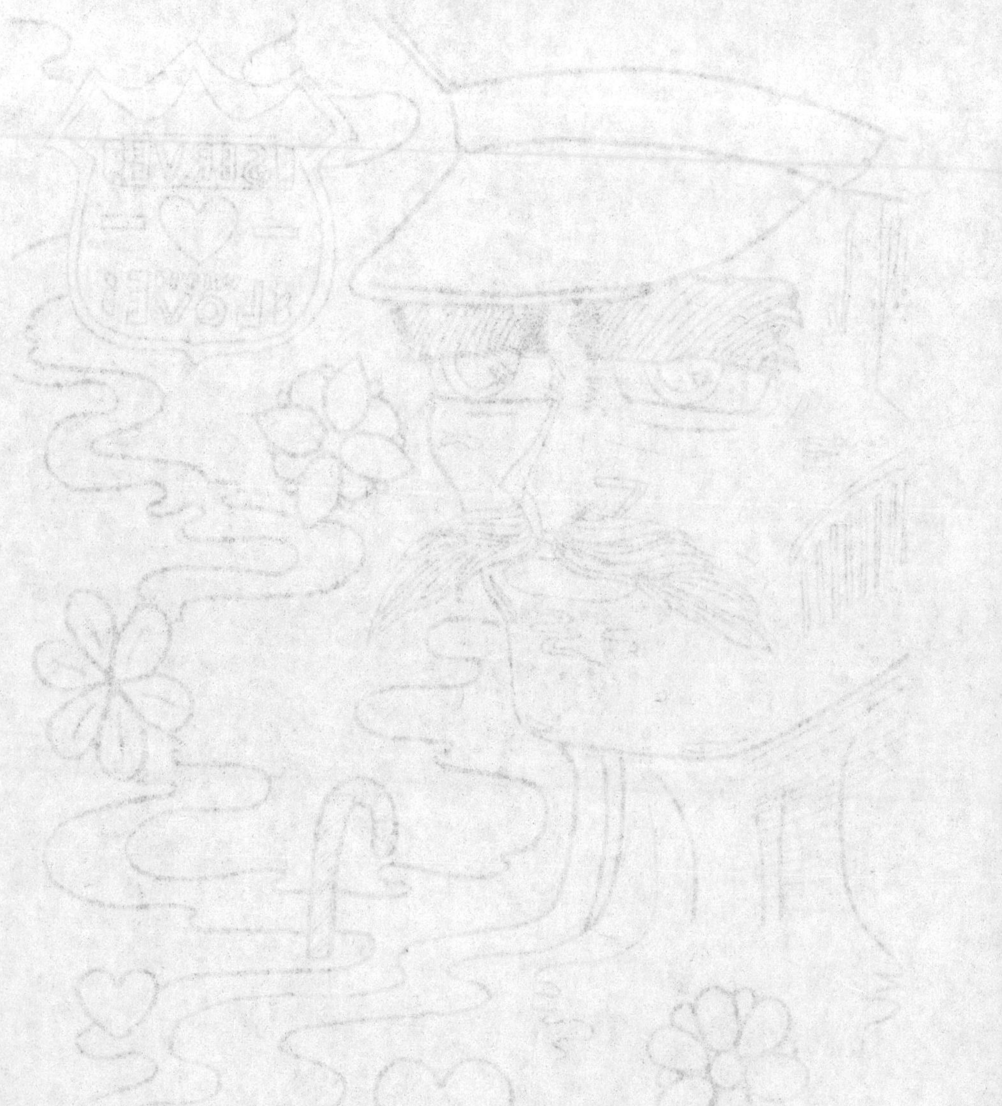

Power

—for Elijah McClain

the Man sprays pepper
calls down Twitter gods
becomes loudest voice
strangles sound from little birds

white hot rage froths
each bully feels bullied
when being called *bully*
retaliate with billy clubs

oh country, my country
peace is a power
generosity is a power
love is a power too

each a gift of glass
delicate sheets
transparent, deadly
when twisted to exclude

you are giddy
overconfident
numb to reason
silent to emotion

power is privilege and music—
violin strings massaging biceps
    sing sweet security by candlelight
—but you contort them, suffocate the gentle

walk back to work
every day. untouchable
bear the weight of conscience
bare the fragility of skin tone

If you feel ready to cast your vote and try making a difference, go to page 181.
If you need to take your spaceship to some big picture windows for some deep breaths, go to page 191.
If you'd like to spend a little time in scripture to re-center, go to page 215.

less twisty

Cinnamon Pandemic Summer Straight

are we here yet? / no? we ate the marshmallow / too fast. UN says / eat those wilting veggies. / methinks we have impulse / control issues. ask that dude, / is he Proud or Border / Patrol goon, swoopy / with Trix, no moms allowed. / neighbor wears Red, / Mama agrees the Silent Americans / should protest censorship, / but oh those BLM fanatics / across the river! stop with the paint! / tear gas makes sense / to combat the freedom-works / that are just fire beyond Independence / Day. time is the ultimate infection. / do we go to the woods, / or buy wood? or just lose it, / like Woody in Toy Story 4? / it's our fifthly moonth-adversity / and I'd like to get it right—/ cause that exists still: / we can know things, / research inter webs, / hashtag Godvibes: / did you know there's facts? / provable as farts. / wooden Adam Driver spoon / the gift unto myself / nachosex vibes / hazy tuning fork vertigo now. / what phase is this? / follow the-yellow-brick-what? / past poppies and doggie poopies / the way shut is littered in fad waves, / licking at our toes, pickle popcorn fish: / bike walk, kick ball, loose teeth, / mug du jour, hammock, / hold me closer tiny humans, / kitty walk, Red Robin delivery, / march, double beach, new beds / garden pee, slowly deflating pool, / all Minecraft, umbrella deck party, / the floor is lava, driveway double dates, / poetry zoom, launch books like rocket duds, / dudę won't pee, splash pad, / stop touching me little fries / home slice giant flies / still March / no, with feet / not the month still. or yes? / are we 21 yet? and if we are, / who shattered the champagne mirage I ate for breakfast? / this three shall pass / friends leap off buildings / sheet-capes and Lycra / their invincibility complex / stupidity superpower / plunge into imaginary / herd immunity, still years off / if you can't abstinence / please still use protection / practice safe separation / masks are your best / condom friends. I imagine / thumb wars come November. / banjo picking brains / I'm not dizzy, / you're dizzy / go home inbox, you drunk / filthy full. can has petitions? / ass sweat pretty Rorschach seat / I trip body pool noodle / this time is just hammock / me baby pizza / rock-a-bye taco suntan / I frosting queen / full stop spiral / cinnabon sanity unwound. / eat me backwards right meow / just read the red / hey, now I'm 100 lines if I wasn't loopy

---

Now your transporter will take you directly to The Future, but you have to move quickly as The Future keeps moving forward every second. Go to page 59.

so full of home

Ready to Cast

—for Clara, who recently asked me
why Grandma doesn't like magic

charming two-year-old, tip-toes
—stretch to flip—
everything the light touches is yours

congregate filth, porcelain sorcery
(marvelous twenty-first century)
—twist for purification.

reclining popcorn royalty
reach buttoned wand, jiggery-pokery—
black box bewitched

magicians of my genes fear:
all pointy hats viewed askance—
hide Harry Potter in an attic

acceptable hocus-pocus:
meal-time incantation
over individual tomato soup cauldrons

yet I observe God
stir collective mystic potion—
we drink deep wonder

Jesus invites me to tea
leaves enchanted broom—
together we resurrect

open all closets
illuminate taboo delights—
conjure universal truths

tender fingertips graze
stars shine patterns on palms—
connected we electrify

align crystal humanity
snap sage spell—
turn on our world

send this love from us—
it was here and now—*poof!*—
it is there—

m a g i c

Not Looking Forward to Resuming In-Person Group Gatherings

I like a community
on my deck, Sunday morning
churchers or Thursday night
poets, so many merry squares
of faces on this paper-sized screen
surrounded by succulents and spiders

I enjoy a great cloud
of witnesses in our open plan
living space, observe
me make lunches, kiss noggins
zip up wee hoodies—our cozy cave
always abuzz with action and anxiety

I'm a big fan of control:
camera on / off / flip
to the other side, sneak
some snacks, a quick pee
large yawn, and bra adjustment—
I am magical and momentarily invisible

                    and oh the volume!
sweet happy ears, wince-free
zone where I can and do
turn down the offensive
squeaking, mute my own mutterings
and elevate dulcet prose whispers

I adore a massive table
spread wild with all of the things
that might wiggle into my fidget
space: rainbow squishy ball
chapstick, magnetic poetry, unfinished
to-dos, and three drink options

what joy! the freedom to submerge
my lower half: ride a stationary
bike, shoulders unhinged may confuse
other Zoom room participants,
but here I fly, glorious focused multitasking:
exercise *and* mysticism? yes, please!

I relish this commute:
kitchen to deck, pajama-ed
booty, home beverage in hand
a silent slip to tuck
in the children, no need to coordinate sitters
—I am always *everywhere*

and now I'm told to love
the return to in-person communal gatherings
but these months have morphed me:
cocoon of home is now my wings—
so anywhere I go
this house goes too

Dear Daughters,
After 18 Months of Caution

I filled your backpacks
so full of home

five extra masks
a castle of tiny sanitizers

an entire city of snacks
seeking residence in your body

your water bottle is, of course, a shower
(but please don't dump it on your head)

when you wish for somewhere warm to hide
like the sure safety of your closet floor—

          this hoodie that you refused to wear out the door
is a hug for later on when recess is too cold

that purple ruler is a stairway
straight into my arms

your pencil box is our bathroom
equipped with colorful Band-Aids (but please do not pee in here)

your half sandwich is both bunk bed
and broken locket connecting you to your sister

and if you find some fuzz there by the scissors
I sent you a tiny comfort quilt crafted from your kitties' fur

Love,
Mama

Hungry Doors

stand idling with me
amidst the throng

tuck a tiny nose cozy
mask taut under fluorescent frames

adjust the ponytail again, knowing
it won't last 'til lunch

we ignore the cars, sliding in and out
colorful indecisive Crayolas

it's time for the secret
handshake goodbye:

        each unique, ends
        with a tight squeeze—

when the careful holding releases
we stay, emptied sling-shots

watch: like stones they fly
down the grassy hill

their wind sounds like the decade
whispering behind us: *be safe!*

breathe in for brave
tall final wave at the edge

        and just like that
            observe from this d i s t a n c e

as the summer-famished school
swallows them whole

and they vanish
            beyond sight

into just the vivid recess
of hoping and imagination—

two bright, small sisters
navigating hundreds of strangers

in a fucking pandemic

If you want to catch a ride on a passing Tardis to see the exact moment that this timeline was born, go to page 35.
If you'd derive some cathartic pleasure in revisiting some pandemic home squishiness, go to page 125.
To teleport into a plane of hope and imagination, go to page 243.

wild hairless Sasquatch

Kindred Spirit

—for EMG

few will delight
as much as you
at this *K*-begun poem
eking out geeky patterns
rare souls seek

reverse mirrored personalities
we wave cross-country
seas of land deep as water
Bohemian and iconoclast
bridging heart and logic
leaping from opposite banks
twisting braids of poetry
silk words arching the divide
—mind and emotion—
anchor the ends
        tugging them closer
                balancing tiptoe, marry
cerebral and spirit

weekly we divulge word puzzles, bundle
neatly onto *The Poetry Starship*
cometing satellites with garbled us—
passing phrases like middle school notes, giggling
scribbling margin additions, queries, sympathies

now I wrap up this *K*-poem's suitcase
tuck in secret note to Auntie Lis
expressing gratitude, pleading not too much spoiling
ply *K* with kisses and motherly tears
wave goodbye at the e-station—
hollering to behave, *come back soon!*

Free

—for Bryan

I'm no genius
but these practice rooms draw me—
Kate Winslet draped
dripping inspiration after-hours
half-hearted scales shift to desire
when the last door clicks
and every light extinguished
I will r e l e a s e—
where words are antiquated
be thou my diary
oh instrument of my soul

piano, lead my fingers—can you speak
this angst to sound?
squeeze simple dissonance
between the white spaces
listen for heartbeats

less than soundproof these seventies
carpets magnify my timidity
brilliance doesn't live in fear
but I do.   drift shyly on ivory
until card slot beeps permission to outsider
quickly I pretend "music" again
resigned to remain   u n r e s o l v e d

slowly packing up, I linger
          breath held—hopeful

will the rhythms that reach me
be Sato, Reese, Mehl, Martin
Flores, Vogel, Tippin, Brittell?
arpeggios sharpening skills
to which I'll politely slip out, unsatisfied

or as Free's familiar pounding
escapes thin paneling—I'll slip
puddle under piano bench
feel myself unlock
his songs, catharsis:
            his hands key my release
                        his voice allows my forte

---

seventeen years later
I guess what I'm trying to say is:
do you have a Patreon account?
I owe you for those free private concerts
you didn't mean to give me

Forever Strange: *A Love Poem*

sometimes I blink
briefly blurred

reality slides
a wink of multiverse

nothing is known
familiar, but foreign

this human / being
walks beside me

and I'm like:
who even *are* you?

a stranger I've bedded
this basket of animated flesh

neurons fire randomness
I cannot predict

I know I know you
barely at all

search your face for clues
while you slurp up peach

juice running down your chin
wild hairless Sasquatch

bent over dabbing
forever with that hanky

perpetually in your pocket
even in this middle realm

—but you aren't ninety
you're not even forty—

which makes me want to know
you, fantastic, feral creature, even more

To read more about this fantastic, feral creature, go to page 35.
If you enjoy day-old jelly donuts, go to page 67.
To play a high stakes game, go to page 201.

my spiritual patronus

Relative Mass: An Electoral Lament

ballots cast
like dice dropped hot
rattle in that box   they rumble
eager to be heard
Clark County, Camas
inside metal, each campaigns
makes wagers, boasts—
secrecy envelopes disrobe
place bets on the races
scramble for allies
hoping to stack tallest
first Tuesday in November

one thousand miles east
where the cutthroat trout play
early voting is in full swing—
but these ballots are chill AF
no preening or cattle calls
edged in Yellowstone gold
confident three-pound envelopes
hang back at the bar
sipping top shelf tequila, secure:
when *they* are asked to speak
        everyone will listen—
beautiful, sparsely populated Wyoming

my scream is your whisper
breaking my box
vocal chords shredded
decisions are made
before my coast is reached
        before my envelope's breached
                before my ballot's released

so when you say
every   vote   counts

I believe to my core
Uncle Sam doesn't care
quite as much about me

        this is personal—
        I won't poker face

The Gift of Interpretation

yes, I'll sign that petition
no fan of Epiphany Day insurrections
can't stomach the death penalty
these digital signatures
are quite literally the least I can do

oh, I see you are grateful
and could I also save some tribal land
from Big Oil? it would be my delight
and honestly, yes, I will sign
a dozen more e-documents

and then plaster my social feeds
with research and rage—
wait for the inevitable relative backlash:
my self-erasing Insta-story
striking raw Jesus-nerves

but I am a Quaker mystic bleeding heart
still following Jesus's lead—you know, giving
exactly two shits about religious capitalism
instead determined to feed the needy from thin
air: fishes, loaves, and medical care for all, bitches!

so I stutter scream, speaking in sacred tongues
hoping there's a progressive in the room with the gift
of interpretation to eloquently shift
at least one brain spark. to be clear:
righteous swearing is my spiritual patronus

and I'll set her loose like a prayer
singing praise to equity, casting out
demons of privilege—I can minister too
push the balance of power toward Love
and between outbursts, I'll suck

on CBD and be a "good girl"
adding my name to hopeless causes
stubborn as that one guy who refused to stay dead
and sometimes lost it, futilely flipping capitalists off
their marketplace games while setting doves free

After the Divorce

I still find Jesus
to be helpful, the love
pouring out when he plays
with the kids right
there on the floor
and how he never blinks
when he listens
even though I've been
s i l e n t   for years

people ask how we can still be friends
and then I'm sure you never met him
never peeked between the politics
and pages, witnessing his naked torso
the truth of his incomparable compassion
and never saw the two of us
wrapped together in my bed, falling
asleep each night grateful, you didn't
notice how we lit each other up
Christmas trees flirting with impropriety

of course I know I sound smitten
still giddy in love, and I am
broken. I knew I had to share
him with the multitudes, but recently
that has become impossible—
the trash he comes home with
the baths I prepare to restore him
how he keeps going out
anyway, it's his nature to try
saving the most egregious
                    the most distraught
                              the most violent

and this is how he set *me* free:
telling me *yes*, seek
the companionship of *more* gurus
—he did not fight for custody
of my soul, it's mine uncontested
we'll still spend most Sundays catching
up, along with the occasional midweek
family dinner, we're determined
to stay in touch and always look
for the best in each other

in fact, on Wednesday, Epiphany 2021
when I finally signed the papers
and he carried out a box of childhood
Awana badges, he gave me a gift:
his beloved Rolodex
(which has since been digitized)
containing the personal email addresses
of some first-name-basis type friends
he knew I'd want to spend some time with:

Saint Nicholas
    Samwise Gamgee
        Shonda Rhimes
Sirius Black
    Snoopy
        Socrates
Sonia Sotomayor
    Stacey Abrams
        Steves, Martin and Colbert
    Swami Vivekananda—
and that's just a sampling of the S's

Continue studying the "S" section for "Systemic Sins." Go to page 215.

view from my window

View From My Window

:: Bedroom :: Lincoln Street :: Roseburg, Oregon :: 1992

she leaves the TV on
all the days of our lives
and for each of the twenty-two
cats' nine lives. if I crane

my body, just so
across my built-in
double bed, I can squint
see tiny technicolor

practice bad lip reading
until queen feline fills
windowsill, gray fur
spilled in sunlight

she collects raccoons too
the always full dishes
out back attract Oregon
cast offs. one summer

striped family of six
moves in. we hold our breaths
watch them try to locate
entrance to garage: tubing

which lets cats walk the air
house to garage and back—
my box fan blows so much that year
removing skunk stink, blocking

bedroom screen time. I fall
asleep scared of fire, strategizing
three stories over driveway:
pop out screen; toss photo albums

first; then every blanket, pillow
hundreds of plush friends
onto the van, *L E A P*—
other times I listen to crickets, dream

about that pink house:
all of us cats with evil twins
pregnancy scares, drinking
wine and slapping skunks

View From My Window

:: But Actually the Front Door :: Lincoln Street :: Roseburg, Oregon :: 1993

the future smells like a decade
of dust, twisted metal, rust
and pavement during summer's first rain

unfocused for hours—or a minute?
does time make sense? my view
becomes purely inner landscape

the silence buried inside cricket buzz
electricity chirping lines of infinity
looks like triple-mirrors folded
into triangle, my face coned
inside, repeating beyond crystal seas
sanity teaspooned in self-miniaturizing release
but how to reenter?

the luxury in retrospect
to criss-cross applesauce
by the screen door

nose turning tiny
mesh waffle print
thinking of nothing and

e t e r n i t y—

why did I do this?
more importantly, how
do I convince my children to do the same?

View From My Window

:: Front Window :: Lincoln Street :: Roseburg, Oregon :: 1994

the perpetually floral couch my perch
hours of reading and fake napping always
turn to genuine sleep, slow waking

shift dreams to that delicious masterpiece
front window frames Roseburg rural
pretending to be urban, becomes neither

humblest landscape, hillside dotted
little 1950s dwellings, each pastel, rising
beyond Mama's front lawn Easter tulips

I remember the grass faded sage, but I know
every summer it browned at the edges
lemon birthday cake left in the oven too long

across the street: quaint blue cottage
inside the elderly couple who would die
                    within a month of each other
leaving lemon drops and a wiener dog named Sophie

the rest kept mysteries, blowing my mind:
how much depth of humanity could each hold?
          was anyone staring out their window
wondering about me? crafting my world?

two-thirds up the hill, right of center
my favorite yellow house rests
                    a stick of butter, soft
and warm, no matter the weather

that's where the heart lies
          if I could cut to its mysterious center
I'm sure the whole universe would slide
into mouthwatering, resurrected focus

View From My Window

:: Newlin 2 :: George Fox University :: Newberg, Oregon :: 2004

we are framed
for display

bold picture window—
we never close the shades

stones throw from Bauman Auditorium
musicians and chapel-goers flow

steady trickle sliding down
our narrow side-street view

consider us campus performance
artists, always at play

the opening act
to wherever you're heading

we're not constantly surveyed
but the game is ever on

peekers, guests, patrons
oh! what you see:

        Tupac presides over stereo
majestic blocky speakers stacked akimbo

above hangs kissing maracas
adjacent tumbling shoe pile structure

        Marianna's in the corner
waiting to be turned on

and over the broken couch
        the holy repetitive futility

splashed citrus ecclesiastical skeleton
eyeing Uma Thurman bedpan canvas

overhead, proud spaghetti sticks
next to Twister board kitchen entry

        spin to reveal the correct limb
to breech the space where snacks abide

below Marianna's Star Wars skirt
craft paper peace pipe presides

giant box TV partially blocks in-lookers
backed against the window

get close enough and you may hear:
Doctor Mario sorting capsules

Wayne adventuring
Bill or Ted exclaiming

dudes and dudettes
the center of this installation is *living*

we flow in and out
yoga, pranks, homework

underwear tank top
artists create, plot, guffaw

flaunt our heretical thighs
proud panties (particularly during chapel rush)

If you'd like to enter the holodeck and find a nudist's forest, go to page 27.
If you'd like to enter the holodeck and continue exploring college, go to page 171.

gripped in denim
squeeze

Parenting

B	I	N	G	O
emergency C-section slice, stretch squeeze, startle snuggle & stitch	glowworm super cool sunglasses cozy warm NICU baby	urine fountain in your mouth	repeat reheat same coffee 12x in one day	your favorite shirt splattered baby poop pattern unnoticed by you four hours
happy, pudgy fists burrow deep then plunge toothless mouth full of sand	rainbow of Play- Doh caked dry in hair	two kids two carseats two poopy diapers side by side	clock strikes midnight: offspring upchucks	creak of door eerie moan like ghost, long white nightgown terror stalks the halls pre-dawn

forgot to diaper toddler before bed— morning is a puddle	Halloween costume home-constructed with supplies of surplus: TP, TP rolls now empty &/or diaper boxes	NO FREE SPACES IN PARENTING —— stepped on Lego, swore like sailor	child suddenly sounds stuffy at lunch: tweeze raisins from nostrils	green peas spiral inner conch of preschool ear looking, yes just like marbles in a funnel
first deep clean of car in 6 months discover backseat marker mural	save your energy surrender this battle: sticker swarms now cover every dresser	attempted escape velocity thwarted when shoes refuse to fit: pull out two plastic princesses & a Matchbox car	rearview mirror displays toddler waving sweet potato fries dangerously near current carseat blowout swamp	preschoolers bicker over magnets while you pass out in the recliner: and / or : now you have three kids
take a single night off spouse says yes to silly Bunchems tossing— then cuts said toys out of foot long hair	turns out that earwax was a tick head to the hospital to check for Lyme disease	playground visit spawns ER trip to surgically glue child's face the night before first day of kindergarten	listen like sleuth outside bathroom waiting for the sweet, sweet sound of that oh-so-vital pre-bed whiz	change child's sheets 4x in one week

Battery

You're only as happy as your most miserable child.
—Sarah Payne Stuart

endless life would be cool
that green throbbing up at the knobby end
juiced up elixir surging supreme
nerve endings abuzz with buoyancy

then, sure, I *could* leap tall buildings
lasso the sun and go for a whirl
launch exploding bombs beyond orbit
lash melting ice caps permanently back together

instead all I am is depleting
hovering at 57% for hours
and poof! plummet to 1% remaining
in the blink of one mundane minute

fill my home with pristine cords
reminders to plug in
manage my sparkle source
make it smiling to bedtime

fall asleep muttering
failures pulsing, my temple:
jumbled perfectionist grave
begging unknown deities for patience
compassion
creativity

all I really need is infinity-energy

with this flow I would laugh so quickly
love relentlessly, each annoyance a jewel
listen to tiny people stories for hours
without taking bathroom breaks

I would caress sticky tangled yards of hair
lure reluctant minds toward math with mirth
lick the brutal wounds of childhood
lunch on misery and shit out sunshine

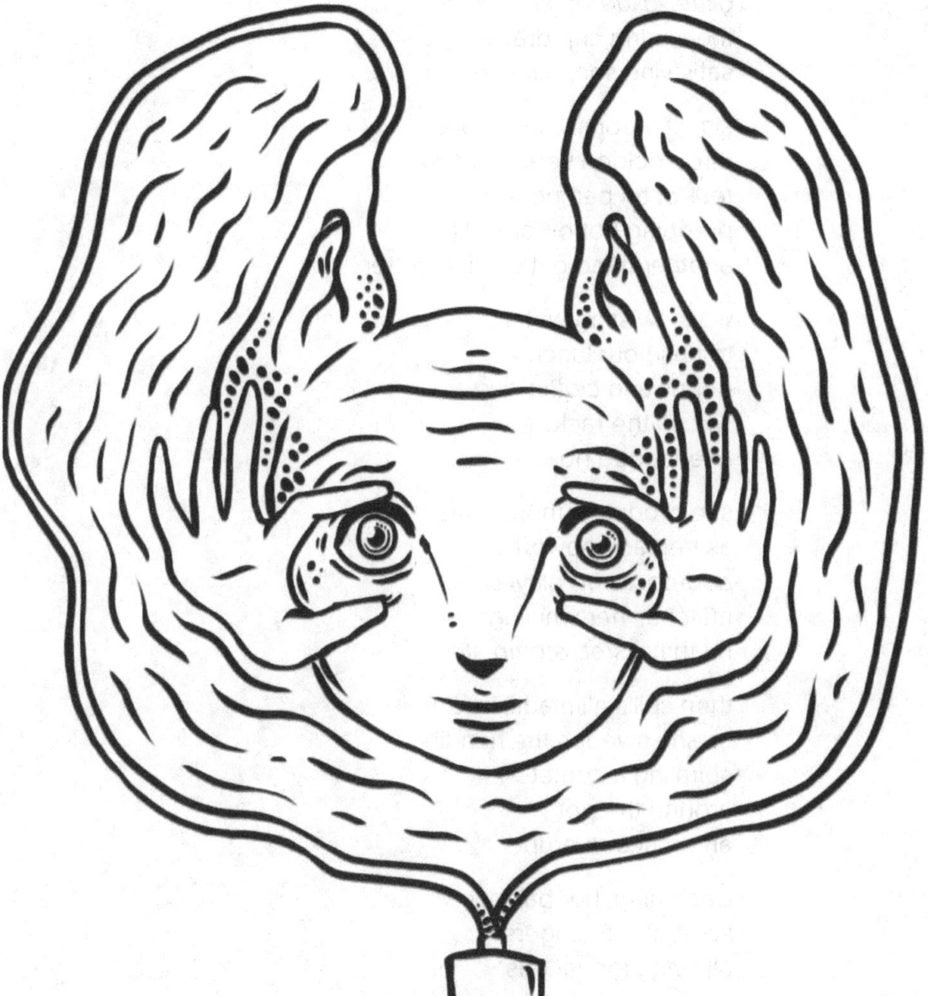

In Case My Children Never Write Poetry About Me*

Mama's hips so smooth
gripped in denim squeeze
glitter-glide-bump to slide
measuring cup drawer
satisfying snap closed

simultaneously she drops
three golden seeds *rattle-*
tee-tat tin pan popper
prepping hot oil, she slips
another hand out to slice butter

while twisting water
to rinse our lunch
debris and *clatter-sud-*
splash the rack
overloaded now

she produces more arms
as her lady powered
pop-pop-ping playlist
matches her whirling
rhythmic *step-stomp-step*

then spills all magic nuclei
as she sweeps the handle
spiraling a comet
around the pot
an orchestra erupts

deafening, her balance
so tight with fingers
all flying for various
perfections of order
as chaos consumes

we clamber on counter
bowls outstretched
oh-mama-mother-dearest!
our pleases assuaged
when her brief-as-lightning
amusement strikes silly
and those endless limbs toss
salted perfect puffs—such rain
punctuated by her laughter
pitter-patter-plunk floor scatter

oh storm of good humor
we embrace before the sun
burns her out to blistered husk

* I wrote this after reading another poet's beautiful poem about their mother, and, having already written about my mother a little, I wondered if my children would ever write about me. I decided I could write about me from their perspective. I didn't show it to them or tell them about it. Two days later my oldest child, eight years old at the time, showed me the following poem that she'd written about me and the croissants I had made on a recent snowy day. Turn the page.

Croissants

by Clara Boswell

warm pastries formed by dough
refrigerator keeps them frozen
in the tastes of time
hours later you take them out
roll the slender dough pizza
find the brown goodies
hide them in delicious treasure chest
and place them in a burning-pastry machine

I bite into the moon-crescent
descender of your creativity
the crispy bread
once dough
now being eaten
by us

Caretaker

If I'm shining, everybody gonna shine.
– Lizzo

she left this for me
where I couldn't miss it

city of medication bottles
rising whitewashed towers

edge of the counter
they form a remarkable grid

I make each capsule a car
before the inevitable airplane

landing—note my cup is full,
always full—she never misses

anything: lunch plated
laundry sorted, books stacked

at the right angle, in the right order
on the sunny corner of my desk

I find a want and turn
seeing it's been met

already—while digging
for impossible to find snack bowls

violent popping pulls my gaze
to stovetop where it's all arranged:

napkin, chocolate, elusive bowl
condensating iced coffee

such intimacy, this intention—
I'm floored when microwave beeps

another reminder that she cares
enough to know my desires

and runs before me
                    a time sprite

fluffing pillows, spreading blankets
forever a step ahead preparing

my comfort for after I have fairied
all of the things for our children

I'm high on gratitude
tears form

finally sit to bask
in this perfect care

and thank myself
for not forgetting me

Congratulations! You have found a pocket of magic. Hold on tight as you tesser to page 159.

a donut and community

Generational Curse, a Slippery Slope

An undeserved curse never alights,
like a wandering sparrow, or a swallow in flight.
—Proverbs 26:2

Our ancestors sinned,
but they are long since gone.
Now we are the ones who must bear
the burden of their guilt.
—Lamentations 5:7

guilt is stacked
shoulder to shoulder
a gilded responsibility
to each child born

we hold the burden of atrocities
ancient bones committed
how fair is it: this shame
rolls down, like inheritance?

surely this land belongs to the children
of conquerors: this is our birthright
but we only accept positive payouts
reject the other edge of privilege's sword

as blameless as bootstraps, we've been taught
so many ideologies and adopted them as our own
re-dressed for this century
(if the aggression is micro, is it still racism?)

nepotism is a slippery fish
culpable progeny swim the same streams
Jesus symbols tattooed on tails
(if the land is promised, can we get away with murder?)

this curse sticks, passing
from parent to child. each tastes
sour grapes, calls it fake news

(would a lie by any other name taste so sweet?)

obstinate offspring systemically obey flag
and king and country, further grinding
generational victims—the original perpetrators are dead
(so who will clean up this mess?)

but there is hope still when the youngest refuse
the wine from their parent's table
eat instead the bread of restoration, asking:
what is the next right action?

Antler ✝ Flag

all my childhood pastors hunted
proudly singing God battle hymns
teaching us to seek our sin
as wilderness prey, ours to dominate

remember that gun rack—
parked by the church office
framed in pickup truck window:
a casual sigh of confidence

we glimpse the youth pastor
crying genuine tears
each Wednesday watching us
devour licorice and Cheetos

we sense his gratitude
this second chance, his need of redemption
we heard of drugs, mill work
a divine desert encounter

so quick the slip
from fear to belief

I forget I'm being watched
but he *still* calls me Sweetie
on Facebook birthdays
says he's proud of me, *kiddo*

I'm out in the woods
when he rustles again—shoots me
that viral video from the '60s
warning of "race equality"

"socialism disguised"
it's just "communism in camo"

this all threads together:
taxidermy, crucifix, and country
a corpse of faith
shackled to fidelity

now he prays for me
and I weep for him

LORD

with every utterance
of that word p i e r c i n g
my ears, sharp and heavy
I must physically heave
shoulders U P under *that* weight

balanced there, pause—i n h a l e
hold *him* uncomfortable
unwieldy—unconscious to all
else while *he* rousts, bloody
bluebird failing at innocence

suffer that word's history: s t r u t t i n g
neglect, improper ordering of human
dignity and decaying other-deprecation
seek any Light remaining in this language
finding none, finally e x h a l e—

throw back shoulder boulder
let it r o l l down my back—
as this is Sunday morning
          brace for the next wave
hope to hear some Good between

it is not this way for all
some let it f l u t t e r overhead
or welcome the crashing wash
as this title crafts their countenance
          they revel in the alteration

I do not have to s t a y
but perhaps I am stronger
through this particular practice
power in mindful non-participation
character chiseled by resistance

Collection

how long have I left you
sitting there, plentiful dust
like so many Sunday morning
megachurch congregants?

you are a nine-car pileup
I-5 traffic instigator
precious debris s c a t t e r e d :
quarter portions of donated

day-old pastries, programs folded
like fans, pencil shards, felt Jesus
and donkeys lounging on plastic
palm fronds, Nilla wafers, tiny stacks

teetering purple-tinged communion cups
buckets of red licorice, severed
foosball players, red letters s p l a y e d
o p e n for pap smear annual exam—

all smug before, now you c o w e r
back row garaged bookshelf
each a time capsule *twerking*
(as modestly as possible)

eager as history to revive my memories
these B - I - B - L - Eees haunt me:
pink patent leather Precious Moments
prized first (pairs well with saddle shoes)

splatter-paint Teen Study Bible, fortune
taped on cover: "Happy news is on its way to you"
Grandpa's navy blue King James, just one
verse highlighted, "You cannot serve both God and money"

The Message, silicon green, smells
like My Little Ponies. handful of Gideon's
take themselves too seriously
(multiplying myth / history hybrid-bunnies)

two red show-offs, golden
edging, engraved for me
the insides crowded like diaries
(bubble lettering: testament

to two-year discipleship intensive)
and still more, silver and cerulean, unremarkable
reminders conflating nostalgia with worth
too much collateral damage   and y e t

the people packed in your pages still
hold promise. sacred interactions
precious friendships. I can't stomach
throwing them out with the holy water

so I   l i n g e r   in the wreckage
sifting what's salvageable—
Easter pageant pre-dawn preparations
a donut and community

Spark

before I've even begun, I know
this poem will drift into cliches
the majesty of the mystical
is vague by nature

elusive buttercup caught on the breeze
hint of yellow pulling my peripheral
that divine lemon flash
all around and never fully digested

this is a thank-you
to small town Christianity
training wheel structure
teaching basic appreciation for the soul

ghostly goddess, so shy
had to learn all the rules
oh the game! endless hide
and seek! such simple guidelines to start:

the answer's always Jesus!
my love for humanity began there
tender golden sprout sneaking toward Light
learning songs and compassion

we all thought I was daffodil
honey-sweet, simply following
sun-patterns etching sky laws
—but I am Lightning

startling champagne promise
—we're all so much more
free once we know
which restrictions to break—

no child is meant to crawl forever
clapping merrily along to the service

so, again, thank you Sunday School
for the gilded maze and Nilla wafers

my spirited flight
launched in your snug walls

Launch sequence cannot be stopped once it has begun. Go to the next page.

Divinity is a sneak

Belonging

we thrash—
toddlers spilling
emotions like warm
milk flung from sippy cups

splashing walls
painting the floor
with slippery ennui—
outside the steeple stretches

elegant Goddess
draping our tantrum
with patience
she smiles

door-mouth wide
swallowing each ultimatum
we waltz in, clutching
precious sorting boxes

and label makers
—so tiny, we are
kittens lapping confusion
onto pink tongues, the mingled

flavors don't make sense
we want to separate
sacred contradictions
—I am one

with the three-
year-old crying
I am not a number!
I struggle to fit—

my shape wants more space
she was a tree
before we made her "church"
in silence she learned

the nature of things, now
she stands witness
to our similarities spreading
thick like constellations

spiraling all of our DNA—
earthlings too focused
picking out differences
like bad apples

she cradles us
Sunday morning
time-out turns nap
we all become

c o l l e c t i v e

Saltiness Restored

—for 13-year-old me, taught to be scared of my own body

> You are the salt of the earth; but if salt has lost its taste,
> how can its saltiness be restored?
> —Matthew 5:13 (NRSV)

lick me
I am stone
found worthy only in stillness

maracas abundant
burlesque, told *don't*
look back. your future is fiction

shackled by fear
these salty ladies freeze
pillar-wives of Lot

my shakers are shapely
smooth curves
warm to the touch

Shakira takes chisel
stifled shimmy revives
we join J-Lo

shake it all out—
these centuries of underwire
long underwear, bloomers

        layering modesty panels
board shorts and baggy T-shirts over
one-piece bathing suits

halftime social media aftermath trampling
deepens my sparkles
gyrating into freedom

Cling

slippery memories drape
        sheet-like over furniture
        create sticky mausoleums
out of half-chewed pencils

and worn-once onesies
        rosy rearview past leeches
        future out of present, like color
sun-bleached away on the line

nostalgia-infused items linger
        paralyzing generosity, I
        grip clothespins, rail
                against impermanence

wrap finger strings tighter
        hoard fear like clearance
        dryer sheets I don't even want—
three friends are pregnant

first babies, my heart
        retreats, eyeing our crib
                (teeth marks from two
        the last, more content

just waited for morning)
        capitalism whispers
        w h a t   i f   ?
implying resurrection of need

hospitality replies
        w h a t   i f—
        we all open our homes
like libraries? free

membership for all—exchange
        as often as circumstance
        and reinvention desire
buy nothing

as often as possible
shake dust gathered
from the storm of too much
relax curled yearning

from clothesline plenty, clip
compassion like lawn art
flapping in the breeze
signaling red carpet reception

replace belongings
with snug connections
—shift loved items
to new loved beings

trust my own welcome
when evening winds ease

My Favorite Pronoun

Divinity is a sneak
—we know this
mischievous Puck*
dancing fairy rings around the periphery

we like to scan
the puffy face of clouds:
is God there?
benevolent, bigger than myth?

peek under granite
stone-countenanced
and still, like moss:
is Creator there? patient and unmoved?

peer at that old rugged
torture device: is there relief
in that infinite Spirit
that eternal pain?

and while we seek
this Glorious Lurker performs
delicious acts
of demonstrable kindness:

doorbell-dashed roses and tea
pancakes shaped like Mickey*
colorful quilt tucked all cozy
a clean house

we flutter, so busy
looking up and down
these gifts appear
like miraculous ancient manna*

but if I level my eyes
become present
I see so simply: we're the Ones
we've been waiting for

just below each pore
delirious Mystery
a grasp of Glitter
always available

the sacred Spark is *here*:
my favorite pronoun
for the unexplainable
                                        is you

* popular well-meaning prankster character in William Shakespeare's *A Midsummer Night's Dream*
* Mickey Mouse, Disney's lead character and logo
* Food that God gave the Israelites during the Exodus

To encounter a sacred human, go to page 67.
To seek the sacred within decay, go to page 77.
To bear witness, go to page 145.

tumble like lumber

Entmoot

behind the bark
our sap begins to boil

already machines of war
slice my neighbor's roots

the world is changing
limb-lithe littles

climb up higher
my crown is full of whispers

ancient secrets growing
forever, like my name

wreathing my trunk
beard of watchfulness

I am old—
and you are very small

but perhaps together
we can *boom-ba-room*

with doom for destruction
shout *stop!* and mean it

shepherd Earth beyond
bickering undergrowth

somehow, like downhill
resist hasty hellos

teach the evergreen
art of intention

leave legacies
Merry and Pip—

            branch out
a little more wilderness

our saplings must
be friends—

survival demands
these shared forest songs

Quench the Mystic

underground swells universal river
global life source prolific—
we drill to find
numinous expressions nuanced
necessarily by point of entrance
each pump seeking ultimate
t r a n s c e n d e n c e

my buckets came from church
labeled for the *one* fount
from which it sprang. only
I thought to find depths, I must
stay, avoid the shallow
of t o o m a n y *other* swallows

decades of drinking, I am not drunk
yet from enough d i v i n e

have I tapped out this well?
are the dregs worth lingering?
cup quite d r a i n e d

how can I remove these walls?
let the water flow unhampered
aquifers a b u n d a n t

let the source mix
collaged divinity
I'd like to straw
these truths
t o g e t h e r

mingled flavors compliment
Buddha, Mohammed, Christ, Picard
all share their favorite beverage

I taste them
g r a t e f u l

Mother Winter

I love this time
sky dome sleepy

when Mother pulls
down the atmospheric

shades, we're drawn too
into effervescent dusk

the mountain-sill is lit
thin line oversaturated

pale pink and clementine
she does this on purpose

leaves peaking space
(closet door cracked—

Mother likes a sneak)
pulls   f o c u s

to the perimeter. we come
together, attracted by Light

this is her way
of putting the dogs out

shuttering distractions
inviting us all inward—

we remember our roots
lure us home, Mother

Dune Climb

kelp clumps litter shoreline stroll
to driftwood play structure summit—

the Pacific carried this oak
how far? from which cliff did it leap?

now beach-embedded, blackened
by sunset bonfires, crustacean

graveyard. all that glitters
crushed by sea, sand-sparkles

ascend coastal belly
steps slide a little each lunge

shadow shoulders heave—
breathe, loud atmosphere chorus

gasp peak panorama viewpoint
wind treachery attempts assassination

grip root, wiggle down leg bipod
hold camera eyes steady—

blink capture scenery, h o l d
steady—ten, fifteen seconds s t i l l

enough to retain the memory
cemented with sand sting

burnt-orange fuzzy caterpillar
passes, already completed sunrise

dune climb, smaller than Herbert's
sand worms. relax calves

carefree, become nature's child
tumble like lumber, gleeful descent

Into the Unknown

—for Teddy

you pull my hand
no, *yank—*
point to the trees:
is that the future?

then toward the ridge:
there it is!
the future!
I want to go to there!

each few steps you tug
such strong grip
hand a third my size
soft as butter, unyielding

run, finger extended
your compass arrow seeks some north:
a pine cone, daisy, dog poop—
are any of these the future?

glimpsing future's elusive shadow
in our fancy grown-up words
as we discuss possibilities
of what we'll find in that magic-

land. in such uncertain times
we must be seeking her
more than normal. you notice
and have joined our holy quest.

dear reader, this isn't metaphor—
how would *you* explain the future
to a three-year-old who finds
only the present wherever he goes?

To quantum leap to the start of the pandemic to see about some sprouts, go to page 59.
To join the holy quest for Cute, quantum leap to page 97.
To close your eyes and feel the pulse in the room next door, shimmy, while turning to page 125.

epilogue

How to Wake

with thanks to Annie Lighthart

It'll be interesting to see how yesterday goes.
—Matt Boswell

sever oblivion with a blink
ride the long dark cord of consciousness
back from the Big Bang
where there's no separation
of self from infinity—sleep
is where we jumble
existence shrugged off at the nightstand
waiting with glasses, Fitbit, and phone

where was I?—swinging
back into me
r e m e m b e r
what me *is*—
grope internally for the lights
and perhaps a wee
cup of Jo—there she slips
into focus, a gasp of personality

hover outside of time
some infernal hang time
seeking the present me—
locate first this room
then the year, and how many
children this me has made
and are any infants
in need of a suckle?

now remember that days exist
and feel your fingers
on that rope, pull up
toward which reality this is:
Tuesday, mid-September—
recognize some mild excitement
and connect that feeling to plans:
today I walk at Round Lake!

this waking complete
leave the string for later
to slide back into blessed confusion
after this individualist day is done—
find it possible now to open my eyes
brain and body rejoined
with other sundry bedside items

get up, grateful for the forgetting

Contributors

"In a Twist," "Battery," "Collection," "My Favorite Pronoun," and "Entmoot" by Joey Hartmann-Dow.
All thirty-five remaining illustrations provided by Jay Williams.

Clara Boswell ("Croissants") is a tweenager that likes adding artistic creativity, nature, tropical fruit, and books to her days. She likes cloudy days with a touch of mist and sunshine, and loves reading fantasy, nonfiction, adventure, and sci-fi books. She lives in Camas, Washington, with four humans and two cats (that purr and meow 24/7).

Joey Hartmann-Dow (she/they) makes various work about humans, creatures, the earth, and connections between all those things. She makes drawings like these illustrations, as well as paintings on maps and mixed media. Joey lives in New Orleans, Louisiana and dreams about justice. You can find more of Joey's work at www.usandweart.com

Jay Williams is an illustrator, musician, and weirdo living in Hood River, Oregon. Jay's perfect day is a gloomy one, filled with coffee, books, drag, cartoons, and kitty snuggles.

Acknowledgments

Many thanks to the following publications who first published these poems (some of these have been slightly altered since those initial publications):

"Belonging," "LORD," and "Saltiness Restored"—*Our Church Too*
"Belonging" and "Sexy Stranger"—*Wordlights Radio Hour*
"but if you go too soon"—*VoiceCatcher*
"Casual Caking"—Oregon Poetry Association, *Pandemic Anthology*
"Cling"—*Western Friend*
"Collection"—Not a Pipe Publishing, *Denial Anthology*
"Earthing"—*Tiny Seed Literary Journal*
"Forever Strange" and "Space Bar"—Oregon Poetry Association, *Newsletter*
"Mother Winter"—*Poems to Lean On*
"My Apology to Tonya Harding"—The Poeming Pigeon, *Pop Culture Anthology*
"My favorite pronoun" and "Ready to Cast"—*Soul Forte*
"Power"—*Printed Matter Vancouver*
"protester / police"—The Poeming Pigeon, *From Pandemic to Protest Anthology*
"Venus"—*otoliths*
"View From My Window...Roseburg, 1992"—*CIRQUE Press*

The following poems also appear in my chapbook, breath so hungry, *published by The Poetry Box, 2022:*

Meet-Cute
Fear Flinging Romance
but if you go too soon
Exhalation
Forever Strange: *A Love Poem*

Thank You

Thank you to Lis, who read every single poem before anyone else and carefully gave me feedback. Thank you to Boz for reading them next and replying with heart emojis. Thank you to Eric for close readings and constant support. Thank you to Mareesa for endless creativity and patience. Thank you to the nurse at the ER who asked me so gently, "What's the hardest part right now?" Thank you to Bailey the barista. Thank you to Christopher and Morgan and the Ghost Town Poetry Open Mic community, who heard many of these poems read aloud and cheered me on. Thank you to Jay, Joey, and Clara for partnering with me to create this book. Thank you to Christopher (again), Armin, Meghan, and Megan for offering your written support of this book. Thank you to all of the publishers who published poems from this book in their multiverse, even if they rejected them in this one. Thank you to the #bozzytots (Clara, Renee, and Teddy) for the ways you inspire, challenge, and delight me. Thank you, reader, for adding color to these pages. Thank you trails, americanos, fanny packs, Notes app, Fitbit, rainbow slippers, Gilbert and Carrots, the Daniels, double recliner, fuzzy caterpillars, fizzy waters, tiny bridges. Thank you to countless friends who have gone on walks with me or sent messages back and forth, encouraging me, supporting me, hearing many of these ideas before they were poems, and inspiring me to write others. I hope you see yourself in these pages as I do.

Title Index

A

B

C

S

T

V

W

First Line Index

A

B

C

D

E

F

G

H

I

K

L

M

S

T

U

W

Y

www.ingramcontent.com/pod-product-compliance
Lightning Source LLC
Chambersburg PA
CBHW010051200426
43193CB00059B/2919
* 9 7 8 1 5 9 4 9 8 1 0 5 0 *